How to Pull

How to Pull

A girl's must-have guide to meeting and dating men

TOM KIMBLE

Vermilion
LONDON

1 3 5 7 9 10 8 6 4 2

Published in 2008 by Vermilion, an imprint of Ebury Publishing
A Random House Group Company

The Random House Group Limited Reg. No. 954009

Addresses for companies within the Random House Group can be found at www.randomhouse.co.uk

A CIP catalogue record for this book is available from the British Library

The Random House Group Limited supports The Forest Stewardship Council (FSC), the leading international forest certification organisation. All our titles that are printed on Greenpeace approved FSC certified paper carry the FSC logo. Our paper procurement policy can be found at www.rbooks.co.uk/environment

Printed in the UK by CPI Mackays, Chatham, ME5 8TD

ISBN 9780091922269

In loving memory of Mahatma Gandhi

Contents

Introduction xi

Part One: Basic guidelines of pulling

Survival of the Fastest 3

Always be Prepared 4

Know your Prey 6

Man Profiles 8

Looking the Part 19

Alcohol: Your Fickle Friend 30

The Smile 32

First Contact 35

Striking Distance 39

The Kiss 44

Movie kisses that nearly didn't happen

1: *Dirty Dancing* 47

Part Two: Finding him

Out on the Town 53
Through Friends 58
The Office 61
Personals 64
The Internet 67
Speed Dating 72
Weddings 74
Random Encounters 79
Your Best Friend 82
Valentine's Day 84
Members of the Family ... 86
Movie kisses that nearly didn't happen
2: *Pretty Woman* 87

Part Three: Dating him

Setting the Date 93
The Bar Date 98
The Restaurant Date 103
The Diversion Date 107
The Activity date 113
The Home Date 117
Seven Deadly Sins of Dating 124
Movie kisses that nearly didn't happen
3: *Bridget Jones's Diary* 125

Part Four: Keeping him

Seal the Deal 131
Meet the Friends 135
Meet the Parents 138
The Mini-Break 140
Bonking 142

Conclusion 147
Troubleshooting Guide 151

Introduction

You know you've got it all, girls. You're attractive, kind, fun, intelligent, adventurous, enthralling, sexy, loyal, and, if advertisers are to be believed, deliciously wicked. Even your horoscope promises that the planets are aligned in your favour. Yet your friends still selflessly bemoan the fact that you've failed to secure the man you desire. So what's going wrong?

Are you a victim of false dreams and hopeless fairy tales? Does no one fall in love any more or live happily ever after? Of course, people still fall and stay in love for ever; couples still find each other from the far corners of the earth. The problem is the game just got more complicated.

That is why you need to be fully prepared, that is why you must have every skill and resource within your grasp.

That is why you are reading this book. Sure, you may have taken drastic steps in the past to get the attention of the object of your desire, but you shouldn't be concerned if you feel that you're now resorting to semi-professional advice. Everyone else is, even men.

So what you are about to read is a man's insight into the male psyche, an exposé of how blokes think and act, and a comprehensive record of what appeals to them and what's a turn off. It brings together the wisdom of experience from numerous men who have played the dating game. Some have succeeded, others have failed. All have learnt vital lessons in pulling. And this book spills the beans on all their trade secrets. Fully armed with this information you can go out into the fray and enjoy a much greater success rate.

One thing is certain though: advice on how to pull is no easy task. I suppose it would be easier to say how not to pull guys, since it's peculiarly easy to give poor advice in life. Certainly, knowing what to avoid is the first step to success, but you undoubtedly have the natural instinct to avoid such elementary blunders as referring to the calorific content of a meal, admitting you've been hurt before, crying during Robin Williams films, endlessly telling anecdotes that involve your hilarious ex and taking your shoes off in public when you're drunk (not sure why this one is true, but it is).

But as for knowing what positive steps to take, this can be a bit trickier. Freud never understood what women wanted, men still haven't worked it out, so why should you have any idea what we want either? After all, we sometimes don't. But one important thing to realise is that dating is ultimately just market research for the heart. When companies are disappointed that a new product isn't working, they don't just throw their hands up and assume they are a hopeless case. They improve.

Crude though it may be to compare this process to the business model – after all, romance ain't quite dead yet – it can still be helpful. All success in life derives from kissing many frogs before finding the proverbial prince, but the difference in relationships is that you take each dead end to heart. If you dumped them, you feel guilt and then annoyance leading to disgust when they persist in calling. If they dumped you, you continually question your own shortcomings and debase yourself with those pesky phone calls. And if it just petered out, you feel, well, a little hard done by.

So why is it so complicated? Are men, as you've always secretly suspected, an alien species beyond all rational comprehension? The truth is, they're not. And I should know because I am one. The truth is men are easy to understand, because we're not that different from women; we are strangely similar. (Apart from one key difference: men are not honest and will do anything to pull you if they set their minds to it. Literally anything.) No, it's complicated because both sides are basically scared of each other. Like the two divided groups at the school disco, boys and girls would dearly love to get together, but both factions are afraid to make the first move. Sadly, making the first move is now what you must do, but before you get too depressed, remember it's supposed to be fun.

So what follows is a meandering collection of scientifically unproven tactics to help you seal the deal. If you read this book and follow its advice, you will pull. There's no miracle formula in here, just the collected wisdom of a group of men who have devolved from predators to prey.

The one piece of advice that I won't give you, though, is to 'just be yourself'. That's because 'being yourself' is probably what you have been doing wrong all along.

PART ONE

Basic guidelines of pulling

Survival of the Fastest

This is not a book about science, but it is about chemistry. And I feel that the collective wisdom of those curious, bearded individuals we call academics might for once here be relevant.

You may have heard the chattering classes banging on about the Darwin vs Creationist debate; now whether you side with the intelligent, reasonable evolutionists or the deranged, ignorant creationists (no bias here), one thing is for sure: Darwin must have got laid regularly. For it was he who officially acknowledged that survival of the species depends on the early bird getting the worm and in so doing unleashed generations of screaming hordes at the January sales.

And he's right, God bless him. Striking early is the very best way to get what you want. We know this from every facet of daily life, yet strangely prevaricate when it comes to pulling, as if this fact didn't apply here. And this does not merely mean scouting for the fittest person in any environment the moment you arrive, but also – and perhaps most crucially – moving quickly with the people you know. You find a guy you like, but since you've got such great taste, it's only natural other girls must like him too, so if you don't get in there fast, someone else will. You see, guys can lazily get on the first bus that comes along, even if it's going the wrong way. Think about why you dislike that girl you know who's going out with someone far better than her: it's because she beat you to it. So get proactive. The pulling climate has changed; men no longer hold the reins, so you need to make moves of your own and arrive early to avoid the rush.

Always be Prepared

You're strolling along, minding your own business, lost in your private thoughts about the nature of the universe, the existence of God and where to find decent fake tan. Suddenly a man you know and really fancy springs up before you with a smile and says hello. And, despite the fact that you've actually been hoping that something like this might happen, your heart sinks. You've even gone through this scenario in your head already, but in your daydreams you were wearing that perfect casual outfit, you were bright-eyed and coiffed of hair and you oozed breezy confidence. But today, you're having a complete malfunction. Because you look like crap and your breath isn't too hot either. You were unprepared. Do you surreptitiously reach for some gum, maybe flick your hair into some semblance of order? Or just sit it out and hope he doesn't wonder why you were so unfriendly (not necessarily such a bad thing, as it happens).

This scenario does actually occur with some frequency and in innumerable different situations, for who hasn't bumped into someone they wanted to impress when they were at their least impressive? The answer is obviously not to be wonderful every minute of the day, because that would be a nightmare (for everyone in your vicinity), but to remember that every minute you spend in public is potential pulling time. So bear that in mind next time you're about to nip to the corner shop in your slippers and dressing gown.

And if you really are caught off guard, adapt quickly. If you're concerned that you are so off colour that it will spoil things irredeemably, pretend you haven't seen him and escape. If you're cornered, tell him that you really don't feel like talking. He'll probably be quite impressed and you can later apologise to him, perhaps via a drink. Just don't admit why you did it.

And yet, there is some argument for not keeping up appearances when you're in public. How many people pull when they haven't changed their underwear, when their bedroom is a mess, when they've got something big at work the next day and really shouldn't be going out? In the same way that the unintentional spontaneous drinking session can be so much better than the party you looked forward to for ages, the chance encounter can go anywhere and often will throw up excellent surprises. It's like you've tempted fate. Some might scoff at fate and argue that this merely illustrates how attractive it is when someone doesn't care about how they look, but from my experience, everyone minds, most are just good at bluffing.

Know your Prey

Different venues attract specific types of blokes. If you visit the theatre, you'll meet a certain type (i.e., an intellectual), and if you attend a Capoeira class, you'll meet another type (i.e., a twat). This phenomenon is particularly true of bars and clubs – the place most of us go to pull – because guys like to go on the pull in their own specific habitat. Thus students go to 'nites', media types go to launches, foreigners go to hotel lobbies, etc. So identifying early on where the type of guy you like is likely to be found allows you, with a certain degree of prejudice, to cut out a lot of timewasting.

But I'm not looking for a type, you cry, I'm looking for an individual. And why restrict my options when I might meet someone interesting from the other side of the fence? Of course, that's true. There are pleasing exceptions to the rule, and many people end up happily with someone they never, not in a million years, would have thought they'd like. But the point here is one of probability. You know that there are some people you're simply not going to get along with in life, so it's nicer not to have to bump into them when you're trying to pull.

Anyway, the reason I mention this is that when men and women go on the pull, their usual discernment often vanishes and they go to precisely the kind of places they wouldn't normally be seen dead in. More specifically, the kind of places where complete dicks congregate. Hence you find yourself in an Australian pub chain, a seedy club or meat market, absolutely hating it and wondering how you ended up surrounded by such idiots. Ironically, they are probably thinking the same thing about you. Yet the reason we are all there is the same: impatience. The refreshing alcopop of a quick fix is irresistibly beguiling after a period of thirst. But don't be tempted by these shortcuts. They will only make you feel worse. Make calculated choices about fruitful hunting zones that suit you and you'll be surrounded by the right guys.

♀

Man Profiles – who they are and what they're looking for

♀

The Banker

Telltale signs: signet ring on his pinkie, smart shirt tucked into jeans, foppish hair, sweater draped round neck, squash/golf kit in boot regardless of his age, refers to friends by surname, drinks champagne for no particular reason.

Where to find him: fundraisers, Po Na Na, the most expensive bar in your vicinity, in traditional country pubs, checking on his classic car in the street, military passing-out parades, in hospitality boxes at sporting events, auction houses.

Cultural references: Wham!, James Bond films, *Financial Times* and *Daily Mail*, *Gladiator*, airport thrillers and horror stories, erotica (it's not porn; it's art apparently).

How to play him: he's looking for a girl to spend money on, so build strong hips to bear his children, own a pair of wellies and laugh like a horse.

The Media Type

Telltale signs: baggy jeans, white trainers, record bag without records, gigantic headphones around neck, lovingly tousled hair, eternal stubble, a ring on his thumb.

Where to find him: short film festivals, events with live VJs, playing backgammon in a pretentious bar, throwing frisbees loudly in a park, brunching at the weekend, in VIP areas at festivals.

Cultural references: a band you've hopefully never heard of, a cinema 'movement', TV programmes from abroad, his friend's magazine with a provocative title, the *Guardian*.

How to play him: be too cool for school. He needs to be convinced that you're cool enough for him so be surly and monosyllabic – it works for most people. Wear shades unnecessarily and eighties clothes that clash. Be 'individual' looking. Drink obscure beer out of bottles.

Adrenaline Junkie

Telltale signs: chapped lips, permatan, monosyllabic, long shorts and flip-flops all through the year, does Parkour (where the jobless leap over walls and down stairwells and claims it has some deeper philosophical significance). Drinks Pepsi Max, apparently.

Where to find him: Australian pubs, far from a workplace, bars which have unnecessary DJs, bars which are tolerant of recreational drugs, and obviously skate parks, snow drifts, beaches and Cornwall.

Cultural references: exclusively sports magazines about climbing and mountain biking, etc., books about survival, programmes with Ray Mears or Bear Grylls. 'Extreme' music to head-bang to. Videos of off-piste skiers.

How to play him: adrenaline junkies love hard-livin' chicks. Girls who take it to the extreme are their bag. But don't be too intellectual – these guys went to the University of Life!

Jack the Lad

Telltale signs: football shirt, three-quarter-length trousers, shades on an invariably shaven head, sunburn, suggestion of a belly, folded tabloid in back pocket, mobile phone visible at all times, topless without the slightest provocation, tattoo on biceps or calf (barbed wire or Celtish symbol).

Where to find him: Wetherspoons, All Bar One, Ladbrokes, football matches, package holidays, building sites, riots, jail.

Cultural references: *Too Fast Too Furious*, R 'n' B, books by Andy McNab or biographies of celebrities, *Nuts* and *Zoo*.

How to play him: he will appreciate you if you can behave like a man while remaining attractive. Drink pints, be coarse, shout, reveal your intimate bits and he will love you, heck, maybe even fight over you.

Gangsta

Telltale signs: listening to crackly music on his mobile, his trainers/Timberlands are spotless, he never smiles despite his expensive gold teeth, low-hanging trousers, designer underpants, jaunty angled cap, guzzling fast food.

Where to find him: on the top deck of a bus, thronging outside garage nightclubs, KFC, car parks, street corners and at funerals.

Cultural references: none.

How to play him: accept without complaint the gangsta mythology, which requires you to be one of several casual partners and mothers to his children, fly into jealous rages about his infidelity, demand that he spends money on you and encourage him to fight people for you.

The Traveller

Telltale signs: he's crusty, has bangles, bedraggled hair, an ethnic satchel over one shoulder, wearing either sandals or weird rickshaw-type shoes, holding fire juggling apparatus/ didgeridoo, has a dog on a string, little beard, Maori bone carvings.

Where to find him: vegetarian restaurants, hogging whole benches in train stations, public parks where he can practise tai chi with the largest possible audience, squatting down to chat concernedly with tramps, buying local produce, festivals, gate-crashing your party.

Cultural references: his own banal photographs of Third World children, *The Beach*, *The Alchemist*, *The Celestine Prophesy*, chill-out albums, the art of Banksy, ultra-accessible philosophy, his journal.

How to play him: bemoan how superficial society is, complain about money while having enough to pay for his every need, when enjoying a Thai/Indian/Mexican takeaway, remark how much better the real thing tastes, neglect your appearance.

The Shit

Telltale signs: wry smirk. (No one smirks unless they're feeling villainous – you can verify this by watching *Hollyoaks*.) Whereas some men think this makes them look like a cheeky maverick, it is in fact a heaven-sent warning that they are a shit, playing a guitar, offering to give people massages in bars, doing sketches ostentatiously.

Where to find him: everywhere, but particularly in posh hotels, in gyms, working in the bar industry.

Cultural references: he'll claim he loves romantic comedies and chick lit so he can swat up on what you like.

How to play him: treat him with the utmost contempt. It is the only way to evade him. He will no doubt insult you, but you will have got off lightly.

The Drunk Guy in the Disco

You do not need advice on how to pull him. Just open your mouth and he will come.

Telltale signs: he's sweating and he's done a bit of sick.

Where to find him: holding on for dear life to the nearest solid structure.

Cultural references: whatever is playing at the time.

How to play him: clench fist. Ram it solidly into his guts. Run for cover as he spouts forth fresh vomit.

The Jock

Telltale signs: wearing off-duty sports gear, has rucksack with loads of straps, while ordering drinks he makes reference to fluids and rehydration, has mostly male friends, lack of interest in world events, upturned collar, shirt with laddish nickname printed on back, athletic build, cheap aftershave masked by overpowering Lynx deodorant.

Where to find him: outdoors obviously, on all-male activity holidays, on stag nights in Eastern European cities, in pubs with giant TV screens, on cycle towpaths, cheap discos.

Cultural references: pop music exclusively. Probably has a Roxette CD. Maybe some hard rock to keep up his revs on the chest expander. Likes Jackie Chan and Guy Ritchie films. Reads specialist magazines.

How to play him: buy him a protein shake and he'll be yours for ever.

The Married Man

Telltale signs: unlikely to be wearing his ring, but may do so deliberately under the assumption that women love the challenge, unusually confident, glint in his eye, unadventurous hairstyle, lots of flashy electronic gadgets, brings in packed lunch to work.

Where to find him: propping up the bar on his own, on golf courses and business trips, at the school gates, marriage guidance counselling, sticking out like a sore thumb at a disco.

Cultural references: midlife crisis alert; this guy has tastes that belie his advanced years. Nevertheless, has extensive library featuring numerous classics included in the BBC Big Read.

How to play him: really don't go there. It's always a disaster. To say nothing of the other girl you're screwing over, you can rest assured that if he's cheating on her, he'll do the same to you one day.

♀

Looking the Part

CHILLING STATISTIC

33% of models expect you to be as good-looking as them

It's official. Vain men don't want you hogging the mirror or the limelight. Now you can bag yourself a real hunk and feel like you're doing them a good turn.

How can a man possibly give you any credible fashion advice? You, the glamour-puss fêted for your bold style and sartorial charisma! Isn't that a bit like telling a man how to fart or scratch his balls? Elegance comes naturally to you, for goodness' sake. Well, you're right, straight men don't have much of a clue. Most would find it difficult to tell whether you're dressed differently from one day to the next. But we know what we don't like. So here's what we don't like (and a few things we do).

Don't go overboard on the make-up or perfume. Resist the temptation to apply an extra dab or squirt, it won't tip the balance. You never, ever hear a man complain that the girl he likes wears too little blusher or not enough perfume on her neck. But he will notice if there's too much and he won't like it. You see, men aren't Neanderthals – we notice things like grooming. That's because for us, it's a bit like opening a packet of crisps – we feel diddled when we find all that empty space at the top of the packet. So it is with a tidal wave of cosmetics. We want to wake up with a girl who looks vaguely similar to the one from the night before.

TOP TIP

If you have tattoos or body piercings, casually slip it into conversation. Same with cool scars. That way you can do a *Lethal Weapon*-style comparison of body markings, which is highly flirtatious and very sexy. Best not to mention the clitoral ring if you're in public.

Shoes are, subconsciously for men, a coded system to signal if you're up for it. No matter what you were thinking when you put them on, perhaps 'these ones cover my blisters' or 'those will fit nicely into my handbag', he will unwittingly interpret them as one might a traffic light. Turn up for a date in a pair of Doc Martens and he will be sighing into his soda water. Arrive in a pair of fuck-me boots and he'll be ordering champagne. But don't forget with the boots that you must do everything you can to conceal the fact you are wearing socks underneath. So if things are going swell, excuse yourself and remove them in the safety of a bathroom. Nothing shatters the fantasy more than peeling off sexy boots to reveal those monstrosities. Actually, one thing does do more damage. Those tight/sock hybrids that hang loosely below the ankle. The horror, the horror...

When choosing underwear, should you go for black, white, red, grey, big, small, pants or G-strings? To be honest, it doesn't matter what you wear *because guys basically don't care*. A guy doesn't stop to marvel at how festive the wrapping paper is on his Christmas present. To him it's merely a decorative obstacle. He just tears it off. Sexy underwear may be a bonus, like choosing your dream outfit and discovering it's in the sale, but it's not expected. Its importance will emerge much further down the line, when you are doing your utmost to maintain his interest. That said, and there's always a but, there are perhaps some things to avoid.

- *Flesh-coloured underwear is, as you would be the first to admit, mind-blowingly unattractive. Men would rather see you in their late grandfather's Y-fronts than that.*

- *Please avoid chicken fillets if you possibly can. You'd feel similarly cheated if a man removed a bulging, gelatine mound from his crotch before you got down to it. It's a form of fraud.*

- *Don't worry about VPL. Guys quite like seeing a trace of your pants and are mystified that someone would go out of the way to pretend they're not wearing any. Pants are great. Everyone wears pants. Apart maybe from Paris Hilton (shudders).*

- *Be mindful of Hungry Arse, i.e. when your G-string is so far up it looks like it's embedded in your uterus. It's a bit off-putting. Yes, we like your pants but less is more. The faint outline of the elastic peeping over your waistband is rather alluring, the whole thing is not. Rather like getting the punchline before you've even heard the joke.*

Much debated is the topic of body hair. While there have been many attempts to rebrand hairy armpits as sexy and empowering, these have failed spectacularly. Go out tonight with the equivalent of a pair of chinchillas under your arms and what happens? You feel self-conscious, your friends are embarrassed and men are frightened rigid. No, the only people with hairy armpits now are celebrities with a movie/album to launch. (Naming no names Julia Roberts and Beth Ditto.) Even feminists who saw smooth pits as indicative of man's rapacious need to tame woman's nature have now admitted that's rubbish and had a shave.

Yet while caterpillar pits are unambiguously wrong, legs are more of a grey area. That's because the sexes have different understandings of what constitutes the truly hirsute. You hear girls gasp in horror at their legs, saying, 'I can't possibly go out like this, I look like a yeti with PCOS.' Then men have a peek at the aforementioned legs and to them they look as smooth as a glazed eel. The key here is visibility. Like dirty clothes you've shoved under the bed, if we can't see them, then they don't exist. But if we can see them, general wilting may ensue. So the general rule is: try and make your body look as little like a man's as possible. Modern men have enough hang-ups about being gay that they object to cavorting with someone hairier than themselves.

★

CHILLING STATISTIC

99% of lawyers do not like leg hair.

Seems it was a hollow victory for feminists, then. You're right; we are all equal but different. And 'different' would imply you don't have legs like a man.

As for hair downstairs, few girls are content to leave things to run wild nowadays. What nature intended as a sprouting celebration, a hairy joy perhaps, topiarists now trim to subservience with a precision that would make Edward Scissorhands feel proud. Is a trim important to us? Yes, and to give you an idea of how important, you should know that groinal hair is categorised on pornography websites as a 'fetish'. So, if you do intend to keep things ship shape below decks, there are a couple of bewilderingly painful choices: Hollywood or Brazilian. No doubt you've tried them, no doubt they hurt, but no pain no gain, eh? After all, a comprehensive waxing is to the discerning lady what a horsehair shirt and flagellation are to Cistercian monks. For both, the reward will come later. But actually there's no need for the minimalism of the Hollywood or the naked ambition of the Brazilian. Why not try 'the Cumbrian' – so named because it is a partially tamed wilderness with clearly signposted footpaths to your destination. Less pain, less hassle, low maintenance and you can pass it off as entirely natural. So next time you're off to the salon, think British, girls!

TOP TIP

If you're generously proportioned; tart it up, don't tent it up.

Don't bother with fake tan. Not only will other girls laugh behind your back, but you'll feel self-conscious and smell of Rice Krispies. We won't notice if you're not wearing any, we'll think something's not quite right if you are and may ask awkward questions about where you've been on holiday.

Don't fuss about your weight. Easier said than done of course, but guys really don't mind about weight. Seriously. Unless you're freakishly skinny, they probably won't even notice what shape you are. Impossible though this might be to believe, size is of limited importance to us. Men may seem shallow (and we certainly are), but that kind of concern is limited to the most antiquated of men.

TOP TIP

Guys don't know what stretch marks are, so don't feel you need to forewarn him that you have them. Even if he's looking them dead in the face he won't know what they are, or remotely care, so leave them be.

The only people who do mind about your weight are gossip magazines, who need to make money from it. And your mother. Guys don't mind. Genuinely. The only thing we do mind is when you talk about it. So don't bother with a fascistic diet and don't spend your evenings in an expensive gym when you could be out finding someone. And console yourself that if you did go to the gym, you might end up with arms like Madonna's.

CHILLING STATISTIC

66% of journalists are 'wholly ambivalent' about your weight

And they're the ones trying to make a living by whipping up hysteria about it.

Sunglasses are brilliant and have been beautifying plain people for decades. Quite simply, they hide a multitude of sins and it's difficult not to look cool in them, unless you're Timmy Mallett. Sunglasses will intimidate the man you like, which is a good thing, and allow you to gawp at him with impunity. True, if you wear them at night or indoors, he might think you have a sty or a hang-

TOP TIP

Minimise your dietary requirements. Guys dread going out with someone who can't have gluten/yeast/meat. Though he will begrudgingly accept it once you're together, it's a major turn-off if he has a notion you won't gobble anything that's on your plate. So eat what you can, without giving the real reason. E.g., 'Do you know, I think might try the vegetarian option this time!'

over, but at the right time and place sunglasses are your friend.

When you wear tops which reveal your cleavage do not be surprised if our eyes are drawn that way. Breasts are very nice. We like to look at them. We love to touch them. If we could switch gender for 24 hours, we'd play with them all day long (and then lez out with someone, hee hee!), so please don't be hurt when we ogle your breasts like a hunger striker scanning the menu.

If you are journeying to a rendezvous by bicycle, perhaps due to your commendable regard for the environment, ensure that you do not wear your helmet in front of him. No one should have to endure that spectacle. Take it off in the nick of time. The same goes for high-visibility fluorescent jackets and bicycle clips!

TOP TIP
Don't wear flip-flops if you're over 12 stone.

You may be surprised to hear that feet are quite important for a lot of guys – many men have an attraction for them that borders on the obsessive. Well-maintained feet probably come third after clean teeth and shaven armpits in a guy's wish list of female grooming. Of course, we can't really talk; ours look like gnarled seal flippers with boils and alopecia. But don't overlook their appearance. Guys check them out.

And for later in the game… pyjamas are a no-no, I'm afraid. Though you think you look ravishing in them, and though there's admittedly something faintly erotic about them in a pillow-fight-in-the-girls'-dorm kind of way, they have to stay in the drawer until later in your relationship. Go naked or in a vest and boxers or a big T-shirt with knickers: they're a huge hit. Nighties? Hmm, a bit risky. Stick to the safer options.

TOP TIP
Don't let a guy see you floss your teeth. He will struggle to find you sexy thereafter.

But apart from the pitfalls above, you don't really need to bother too much about your appearance. Isn't it annoying when guys say that? But it's true. You should be presentable, of course – even guys will make the effort – but whether you wear this or that skirt or look one way or another, it really doesn't make much difference to us. If he likes you, he'll think you look great anyway, and if he's not yet sure he likes you, your choice of tights isn't going to tip the scale. Only go that extra mile for yourself, for your own self-confidence, but don't waste the effort on our behalf because, to be honest, we probably won't notice. The good news therefore is that you don't have to spend money on too many clothes, the bad news is that you've less excuse to go on shopping binges.

★

CHILLING STATISTIC

99% of actors find wealth attractive

Of course they do, because they need your money to afford them their farcical sham of a job.

Alcohol: Your Fickle Friend

Centuries of boozing has infused into our collective consciousness the concept that alcohol solves all ills and provides the key ingredient to pulling. And this is still largely true. Undoubtedly a drink, if you're of that persuasion, helps things along and quietens nerves. With strangers barriers are broken down, the banter flows freely and doors are opened for all sorts of new opportunities to pull. With people you already fancy, it's something nice you can share together: a bottle of wine on the sofa, shots in a club, cocktails in a bar, champagne in the bath. Lovely.

And with drinking comes delightful tipsiness, that glorious phase when everything makes you laugh, the world is amazing and you are officially the most entertaining girl on the planet. It's just when you get seriously drunk that things get a bit hazy.

And therein lies the untrustworthiness of alcohol. It removes your inhibitions, which is good. But it goes so far as to remove all of them. Which is bad. So that while you may have the confidence to chat up someone gorgeous, dance like a pro and feel hilarious enough to write for *Green Wing*, you also have the confidence to behave like a total dick. And that's when, more often than not, you unravel all the good work you've done. It also makes you susceptible to the following phenomenon.

There's a peculiar ritual that occurs in the last hour of many a big night out. As levels of inebriation surge exponentially, collective powers of reason desert the throng and something horrendous happens. The jumble sale begins and being sober is the only thing that prevents you getting caught up in it. The jumble sale kicks off when couples have now eloped, and all who are left are single and, to all intents and purposes, up for it. It is essentially a free-for-all where you will be pounced upon by every leering, boss-eyed man in the vicinity. Natural discernment is long gone so the men aren't feeling picky as they stagger around like bumper cars, rebounding from rebuttal after rebuttal with uncharacteristically cheerful resignation. At this point, you can assuredly pull, and seek comfort in the mildly sweating arms of anyone you choose. However, you may not want to give your self-esteem such a battering.

So how do you stop yourself making an error? You may want to take a leaf out of the boys' book here and set yourself a quality control marker. Choose someone who only just falls below your standards of acceptability and mark them. When you find yourself quite fancying them at the end of the night, you know it's time to go home. This avoids spoiling your evening any further by pulling someone you really don't like.

So precisely how much to booze – unlike coke at a rock star's party – is a very fine line.

The Smile

'It started with a kiss,' sang velvet-voiced love-hunks Hot Chocolate, but they weren't telling you the whole story. Before every kiss there must be a smile. And the smile is your most devastatingly powerful weapon. It has been so since the dawn of time, since cavewoman first revealed a toothy smirk because caveman's paintings were so crap. From that moment, culture and society have paid tribute to that most simple of joys: your lovely smile. Think of that painting of the famous woman smiling in *The Da Vinci Code* or the timeless photographic portraits of Lady Diana, Queen of our Hearts; it's the smile that embeds itself deep down inside. Why? Quite simply put, it's profoundly lovely. Nothing is more wonderful to a man than if you smile at him. Even if you're a right snaggletooth, smiling is you at your best.

But it's pretty difficult to do. If you smile at someone out of the blue, your natural anxiety is that they will think 'Oh hell, what does she want?' or look away sharpish, for fear that they are about to be strong-armed into the Church of Scientology. Maybe the only people who've smiled at you recently were students with clipboards and coloured vests, asking you for a minute of your time for starving orphans. So smiling at strangers doesn't come naturally.

And if you fancy someone, surely the last thing you would ever do is smile at them? Smiling would imply you were happy, whereas you're both terrified and self-conscious. But force it, tweak those muscles into overdrive. What may feel like the kind of grimace you pull when someone takes too long taking your photo, is in fact you exuding a tidal wave of friendliness, like a dog wagging its tail (though more elegant, naturally).

So how do you deploy this esoteric weapon? If it's someone you work with but have never spoken to, there will be a general impasse until one of you smiles. As soon as it's done though, you'll have the excuse to talk. If it's in a bar, you know the tricks. You look once and catch their eye. You look again to make sure. The next time, you give them a smile and look away. Works a treat. Hopefully they should muster up the courage to come over after that. If they don't, give them another one when you next leave your seat for the loo or whatever. If that still doesn't work, synchronise your trips to the bar. You should start talking at some point. If you're out in public, the slightest shared misfortune can provide the excuse to smile. If you're on a train and, say, a drunk is blabbering nonsense to all and sundry, you might catch each other's eye, exchange a smile as if to say, 'We think alike, you and I.' Quite a good ice-breaker, after which true experts make some light-hearted banter and subsequently exchange contact details.

If, after all this, you're still thinking, no way, you're too self-conscious about it and have a wonky, gap-toothed smile that wouldn't look out of place on the set of *Deliverance*, you can always grin. Yes, poor dentistry is no excuse. Because failing to smile could make you miss out on something big. Just think how many love stories start with someone's amazing smile. Have a quick look at the Encounters section of a free paper. More than half of them say 'to the girl with the gorgeous smile on the 5.48 to Rippon' or simply 'You smiled at me,' as if it were the most extraordinary act of kindness. It's difficult not to like someone who smiles at you, and fairly easy to fancy them.

TOP TIP

A good trick if you're too embarrassed to look someone in the eye and smile is to stare straight at their ear. Like looking at an autocue, they won't be able to tell and you can carry off your most devastating grin without bottling it through nerves.

First Contact

The failure of modern man is not global warming, war or poverty. It's his inability to go up to nice girls and talk to them. There was a time long ago when he did this with the boldness and self-assurance that befits a gentleman, but that was in the days when he had to duel with pistols to get your attention. Now he's more likely to skulk in the corner, avoiding you like the plague, while nudging his friends and remarking conspiratorially how fit you are. Scores of nice men have become cowards. And dumb fools. They really need a kick up the backside. So unless you want to wait until the backlash from metrosexuality kicks in and nice men start being men again, which, let's face it, might take a generation, better do it yourself.

So, if you're taking the plunge, there are a couple of things to consider. First: have your internal GPS switched to its highest setting. You need to be aware of where the guy you like is in the room at all times without having to crane your neck like a flustered goose. You also need to be aware of the exits and all clear passages. This is not excessive fire-safety precautions (though I guess it's a nice side benefit), it's so that you can plan a crossroads where you bump into one another. You see, men are both territorial and creatures of habit, so in any drinking establishment, they naturally have a base they keep to and follow prescribed routes to and from it – to the bar, the loo, pool table, outside for a fag. Once you've worked these out, it's easy to find the most favourable location to stage an encounter.

The direct approach – walking straight up to him and saying hello – really is scary. Take it from us. Those few steps towards you are so pant-fillingly terrifying that we prefer not to take them nowadays. It's particularly difficult to pull it off if someone's in a group, since the body language and mindset will naturally be defensive and exclusive. It's hard to break into the circle even if you know someone within it. To make matters worse, when you arrive all of them fall silent to watch, while a few may giggle. The best approach is to wait till your prey is singled out from the pack and then pounce. And then you need to make conversation that isn't too contrived. It's pretty obvious you fancy him, so saying 'So what are your interests?' seems a little incongruous. A nice trick is to try diversion tactics, like asking him if he minds taking your picture, or a specific question, like 'Excuse me, did I meet you at Tom's the other day?' He's bound to rack his brains and start

TOP TIP

When talking to a guy, do not refer to yourself in the third person.

TOP TIP

Do not bluff your way in traditional male topics. This is, admittedly, controversial territory, but the question endures as to whether it's a good idea to talk football/*Star Wars*. If you like them, then yes. If you don't like them, it will undoubtedly get you brownie points to learn about them, e.g., 'The original trilogy was of course the best, but Yoda with a light sabre was just incredible.' This really will earn serious respect. But best not be too enthusiastic as it could backfire badly. Guys don't like being challenged on territory they feel they own.

asking further questions, by which time, hey presto, you're in a conversation.

If you don't have the guts for a direct approach, you can try that old trick of positioning yourself next to him while scrupulously ignoring him. You can then segue neatly into some light banter of the kind that might go something like, 'Can I borrow your lighter? Thanks, I lost mine in a gun fight on a recent modelling assignment in the Third World.'

This seemingly casual approach is much easier and a more natural way to start the ball rolling. It's the one favoured by males, and they've learnt it from wildlife documentaries. (Seriously. When lions or bears attack humans, they sometimes saunter up casually, quite embarrassed almost, as if they're pretending not to be that interested.) It's a good way to test the waters without wishing to fully commit. How very male, but how very effective too.

TOP TIP
White lies are acceptable when you're trying to pull. Blatant lies aren't worth the awkwardness of exposure, but it's amazing what inference can achieve. You can say things like, 'To be honest I don't do modelling.' A brilliant line. It is valid even if you've never been near a catwalk.

TOP TIP
Do occasionally stare off into the middle distance. This will both unsettle him (thereby giving you the upper hand) and make him think you're really intriguing. But don't do it too often or for too long or he'll think you're weird.

If you don't fancy doing any of the hard work, you can at least make it easier for guys to come into contact with you. Avoid sitting in a secluded corner, hanging out with intimidatingly large gaggles of girls, and standing in a way which prohibits someone getting your attention. Move about a lot, so guys can intercept you, take your time at the bar, stand near the loos if necessary, or hold your breath and join the smoking zones, which throb with flirtation and sexual tension. Do all you can to help the right guys bump into you.

TOP TIP
Do be careful about reapplying loads of lipstick when you go to the loo, as some men think this means you're well up for it.

Striking Distance

So you've got deep into conversation now, you're flirting hard and things are going well. You fancy him and you're sure he likes you too. And now you want to kiss him. This is quite simply the best part of it all, and consequently the hardest part, certainly for a man.

Now invariably a man will want to take the initiative at this point, because no matter how much you have controlled the situation up to here, reeling him expertly in, he wants to feel that *he* has pulled *you*. Such is his refusal to concede any passivity in the enterprise – despite the fact that it was probably you who went up to him in the first place – that he is likely to recoil if you make the first move here. Of course, a part of him will be delighted you've saved him the bother, but if you were to one day propose to him, for the very same reason that he was taking ages about it, a competitive part of him will be annoyed you beat him to it.

And herein lies another of the fundamental principles of pulling men. By all means take control, manipulate him mercilessly, orchestrate every last element to your taste; but give off the impression that it is he who holds the reins and everything will go swimmingly. Just as with young children, if you can implant an idea and make him think he came up

TOP TIP

Give him a peck on the cheek in the middle of a conversation and then move on as if nothing ever happened. This is extremely effective. It's safe enough to not look like a lunge, but it will have the desired effect. He will be aware that the score is uneven and he'll be keen to redress the balance. Great tip, that!

with it in the first place, you can get him to do whatever you want. With ease.

So the way to hold all the cards here is by getting yourself into – or out of – a position where it's conducive to kiss. You're no doubt well trained in this from having to dodge unsavoury lungers in the past, but remember how you made it hard for them – disappearing to the loo and not coming back/clamping your drink to your mouth as a makeshift blockade/saying you were a lesbian – and now do the opposite.

So, there are two aspects to how you manoeuvre yourself and control when you want to be kissed: location and posture. The first requires more work. You will recall how school discos were fraught with smirk-inducing entreaties like, 'Do you want to go outside?' You both knew what it meant and if you followed it was a tacit agreement that you were going to snog. But that hasn't really changed; the fundamentals are still there, with a little more subtlety. It goes from 'Do you want a drink' to 'Shall we dance' to 'Would you like another drink' to 'Gosh, it's hot in here, would you like to accompany me outside to catch some air?' You both know you can break the chain anywhere along the line and it's a way of saying you're not interested without him having to lose face. And it works fine.

But please give us some help! If we're going to kiss you, we need somewhere private. This is not to spare blushes or prudishly avoid PDAs, it's just common sense. It's easier to corner you somewhere where there are dark corners. So if your guy mumbles something implausible like, 'Let's go and check if the kitchen's on fire,' or 'Have you ever seen a total lunar eclipse?' think back to your adolescence and hear the words 'Do you fancy a snog?' Simply agree to his veiled suggestions and go find somewhere else.

Posture becomes important once you've selected a nice spot for it, because how you hold yourself determines whether the kiss will be a lunge or a natural progression. Men need to enter into the Strike Zone before they try anything on. The further into the Strike Zone they are, the less they have to lunge. Remember those awful movie clichés where the woman drops something and as the man stoops to help her, there's a bit of a moment as they look into each other's eyes and realise how close they are. Laughable of course, but it makes the point that if you're close enough to someone, a kiss is inevitable. So stay close and keep your face angled towards him and he'll go for it. If you look at his lips that might also speed things up.

Apart from slipping off somewhere quiet, the most common places to kiss are on the dance floor, in the back of a taxi and while saying goodbye. Each has its own codes and practices. The dance floor is an old faithful and remains an effective means of sliding neatly into a good snog. And you can do it to any song nowadays, instead of having to wait till Bryan Adams comes on and the DJ gets on the microphone to pester you all to get a move on. The real problem is the time constraint. This place has to shut at some point, and if you haven't kissed by the time the music stops and the lights come on, your good work is squandered. And at really crap 'discos' they'll try and play a big showstopper at the end to send everyone home in a good mood and stop them fighting on the way out, so as 'Come on Eileen' blares out of the speakers, you'll be forced into some bizarre conga circle, which expands and contracts like an accordion. That really doesn't help matters. So remember the ravers' adage: speed is essential on the dance floor.

Being in a taxi with someone you haven't snogged yet is a bit bizarre, but if it happens, it's a piece of piss to put right. No doubt he'll try the old 'I'm-just-having-an-innocent-stretch' manoeuvre and put his arm round you. All you need to do is put your head on his shoulder. It's an awkward angle but the jostling of the cab soon throws you back into a loving (and drunken) embrace.

Saying goodbye is quite easy because you'd be giving each other a friendly kiss on the cheek anyway, and it doesn't take much to repeat the process till you get steadily closer to the lips. What is difficult is when he says, 'Can I walk you home?' Firstly, there's a chance he might turn out to be a sex pest. Secondly, you're even more self-conscious outside your front door. And how will you get him to leave? Saying goodbye is the time when a guy will try and push his luck, so have a clear escape plan up your sleeve. Best do it in a neutral place and then make a dash for it, unless you definitely want him back to your lair.

In the embarrassing event that in one of these situations the man you like loses his nerve and reverts to the adolescent question, 'Can I kiss you,' just grab him and go for it without replying. Saying 'Yes, you may' prolongs the agony and he has to make the move under increased tension and scrutiny. Hideous situation either way, but at least you can speed it up.

Of course, in an ideal world there would be no need for this strategy. In an ideal world, your perfect man would sweep you up in his strong arms and kiss you deeply. But this is not an ideal world. Otherwise there'd be no Scientology.

The Kiss

As a teenager, you practised how to kiss, perhaps on your hand, perhaps on a female friend (ah, such sweet memories!). Presumably you've had enough practice to get it right by now, yet it is amazing how many people complain of crap snogs. But in actual fact it's quite hard to be a bad kisser on your own. What makes a kiss bad is when two lips don't really match. The stereotype bad kiss of a washing machine – round and round with loads of drool – would be fine if the other person did the same, after all, I'm sure you have snogged the face off someone. It's merely a question of misjudgement. Both sides need to anticipate the mood and match it. From gentle smooch to full-on face attack, as long as you're both doing the same, it's fine. Sometimes it's just hard to hold back a little when you've been waiting for it all night.

What to do about fresh breath? The prospect of rampant halitosis makes passion wilt faster than a cup of cold sick. You're wise to the whole tongue-scraping wheeze, but after a prolonged evening's courtship, things can deteriorate. Popping in some chewing gum is a tad obvious – you may as well ask him to hold on while you make yourself presentable for a snog. And disposing of it responsibly is tricky. Once again, matching is the key. If you see your man gobbling up some garlic/coffee/ Wotsits, snatch some and get them down you fast. Likewise, use your feminine guile to coerce him to swallow whatever you're having. Drinks smooth the way nicely – it might even give a pleasant flavour to proceedings: just make sure he doesn't have any allergies.

Finally, when a man kisses you, he will try and move his hands down your body in a carefully choreographed procession towards your nether regions. Though he can't necessarily help this, you can stop for a millisecond and feel flattered. He is intensely attracted to you. Then slap him hard. It will do little to assuage his lust for you but will establish a keen sense of who is boss. Then let him have a good grope and slap him again. Repeat until you reach a compromise you are happy with. This cat and mouse game of fondling will basically make him fall in love with you. If he tries to encourage you to grope his nether regions, slap them too. You're a respectable lady, after all.

So these are the vital considerations to bear in mind. You are armed and ready. Now it's time to meet him.

Movie kisses that nearly didn't happen
1: *Dirty Dancing*

It is unlikely that you have not at some point compared yourself to Jennifer Grey in *Dirty Dancing*, perhaps even unfavourably; you're only human, after all. True, she gets her man in the end, but it might easily have been otherwise. This is your chance to learn from the near-fatal errors that could have lost her the man.

Arriving at Kellerman's, Baby exhibits three characteristics that could send any reasonable male running for the hills: poor dress sense, a facile nickname and idolatry of her father. Now the clothing issue is simply one of taste. If you haven't got it, don't worry; someone else can always help out. Just read the right magazines and trust the advice of your target audience; which, I must stress, does *not* include gay males. As for nicknames, they are best avoided entirely. At the age of 12 what seemed quirky and amusing can sound faintly ridiculous at 25. The problem here, though, is convincing your friends to stop saying them in public, particularly when introducing you to suitable males, unless of course you are affectionately known as Hot Lips or The Bike, in which case bandy it about. Lastly the age-old flaw, that of family worship. No doubt you get on well with the rest of your family, on the whole. But always remember that, though you may do so, no one else gives a toss. It is eternally baffling to gents why a lady would ever boast 'my mother is my best friend'. At best, exude mild ambivalence towards your family, for, as Baby illustrates, there is little more unattractive than a girl in thrall to her parents.

So why the hell does Swayze fall for her? Sure, she sorts out all these issues by the end of the film – where we see a scantily clad 'Francis' defying her parents – but how does she cross the figurative – and in a deeper reading, one might argue literal – bridge to Patrick's heart? (Actually, forget that; this is hardly Ingmar Bergman.) The answer, my friends, is of course her masterstroke of genius: offering to be his dance partner. This unwitting touch of brilliance affords her several vital advantages: she has a reason to spend time with him, she wins the trust of his best friend Penny (never underestimate this) and she gets up close and personal with him early on, thereby making the transition to intimacy easier. You might also note that she cleverly enters into a doe-eyed pupil-teacher relationship with him, which some men of limited intelligence (and let's face it, Johnny ain't bright) dearly love. She also shouts at him, which in the early stages of courtship can actually work wonders for creating intimacy. So it is this trump card alone – establishing a shared interest/goal – that obliterates all her other numerous gaffes, apart, perhaps, from 'I carried a watermelon'.

But despite all this, and this is a big but, Baby very nearly loses it at the critical moment, when she tearfully announces she can't face the thought of never seeing him again. This was a really bad idea. If Swayze had been just a teensy bit unsure about her, the game would have been lost. Revealing true feelings in an emotionally charged moment is one hell of a gamble. Think of it as the bouquet test. If a guy sends you flowers it will polarise your feelings for him. Either you receive them with dread or excitement, rarely nonchalance. Same with a declaration of love. It forces the issue of whether you actually like him. So if you're not sure, and a little alarmed, you'll bolt for it. Amazingly she gets away with it, but only because Swayze truly loves her, but nevertheless, you might not be so lucky. So best avoid copying this and indeed her final lift during 'I've Had the Time of my Life', because you'll only hurt yourself.

PART TWO

Finding him

Out on the Town

It is a truth almost universally acknowledged that people who go out on the town at night must be single, otherwise they're just wasting everyone's time. So the beauty of a big night out is that you'll be surrounded by single guys, all of whom are on the pull. What a heart-warming thought, eh? OK, so while a part of you winces at the prospect of guys with that disconcerting, maniacal look about them, remember that they're not all ineligible, and rather like a ripe avocado in a supermarket, they require some rummaging for. You can also rest assured that unseen forces are on your side since bars and clubs are specifically tailored for pulling by simple laws of capitalism – people will pay good money to pull, so the industry will try enthusiastically to ensure you succeed.

So if the stage is set and they're all ready and waiting for you, why is it still so damn hard? Quite simply because pulling this way demands that you chat with strangers – a notion that has filled you with dread since your infancy. 'Don't talk to strange men' was your childhood mantra, for goodness' sake. And your innate shyness hasn't disappeared, you've just grown more adept at concealing it. It's nerve-racking enough being introduced to new people you don't even fancy, so chatting with a total stranger on the unspoken basis that you want to pull them is a new kind of terror, hence the absurd range of excuses you create to justify avoiding it. ('He's probably married/ boring/ arrogant/ busy/ foreign/ transsexual…') So from whence comes this bum-clenching terror? It is the eternal fear of rejection. A stranger has no emotional investment in you, so he could be prepared to dismiss you on the flimsiest of pretexts. But it very rarely happens that someone will cut you dead. Sure it happened when we were 14, but that was only when people were feeling insecure themselves. So being rebuffed is highly unlikely to happen and in the improbable event it does, screw them. Only a bona fide dickhead would ever do that, so no loss.

TOP TIP

If a guy is 'flashing cash' to impress you, bleed him dry. Order the most expensive thing you can, suggest the most extravagant venue, demand luxury gifts. This is your chance to really go to town. He will be only too happy to spend the money since that is how he legitimises his own miserable existence.

> **TOP TIP**
> Avoid men who say they used to DJ. Everyone has DJed at some flat-warming party or their little sister's birthday party.

No doubt about it, the way to pull in bars and clubs is to hunt in small packs. It means that you never have to stand on your own looking like a lemon, you are more likely to enjoy the experience, you have someone who can watch your back and stop you making hideous mistakes or laugh with you if things go wrong. Most importantly, though, you have someone who can help you engineer fruitful encounters. So no matter where you are going, it is extremely important to choose the right companion, because your wingman could be the life or death of you. Here's how to choose.

Subconsciously you've probably already placed yourself on an attractiveness scale in relation to your friends. You've acknowledged that there are some who are more attractive than you and some who are less. When seeking a wingman to accompany and aid you on your quest, always choose one who is less attractive than you. In short: beautiful friend = bad, not quite so beautiful friend = good. Cruel, but true. If you use the more attractive one, history shows that time and time again, the guy you like will fall for her instead. Now don't go feeling guilty about 'exploiting' your less attractive friend; she in turn will have someone less attractive than her to help out.

Don't choose someone for your wingman who's already in a relationship. Though she may wish you well, her heart is not really in it and her patience will soon run out. After all, a full bed already beckons her. A true wingman pairing should be mutually exploitative in essence. You're both out for the same thing, you will do everything in your power to help each other, you will not retreat until you've got it and you're willing to take one for the team.

TOP TIP

Snogging other girls used to be *de rigueur* as a means of getting all the guys to drool over you. While it remains an enormously attractive sight, guys are wise to the fact that it's a clumsy means of getting their attention. It's a bit naff now. Basically, you will attract the wrong sort of guys.

TOP TIP

Girls, please struggle to resist the temptation to sing along loudly together to your favourite songs in pubs and clubs. This is not attractive. By all means hum, but don't expect to be approached when you're belting out, 'It's raining men. Hallelujah.'

Don't be tempted to use a man either. If you're seen out with another guy, whether he be your brother/ platonic friend/ life coach, men will fear the worst and no one will approach you. Occasionally, a male wingman may be skilled enough to embroil himself in a laddish conversation with a group of men, only to introduce you seamlessly into proceedings. For example: 'You guys talking about the match? Yeah, what a shambles. Me and my single sister were just saying...' But this is the exception rather than the rule and they will smell a rat. Men don't talk to other men unless they're after something.

True, being in a pair makes it more daunting for guys to approach. But hopefully they'll be in a pair themselves, and what could be more perfect? You know the drill; you're drinking at a table with your friend. Two guys come up and ask if they can have the remaining chairs. At first, both groups ignore each other, but a lighter borrowed here, a spillage there and some light banter ensues. Before you know it you're getting tag-teamed on a youth hostel floor.

Of course not everyone needs a wingman. But if you have the guts to sit at a bar on your own for all to see, waiting for someone to chat you up, then you probably aren't reading this book.

Through Friends

The obvious advantage of meeting someone through a friend is that he/she can not only give you a scurrilous rundown of his dating history and whether he's worth pursuing, but they will also be able to broker the deal. But, and this is a big but, you must establish super-fast who's closest to your friend: you or the man you fancy. If it's you, then you hold all the cards because you can exploit your friend's loyalty to spy on him and/or bring about the 'chance' meeting, 'Oh, fancy seeing you again,' etc.

But if your friend knows him better, you're in trouble. In fact you're better off not admitting you fancy him, because they will tell him straight away and you remember full well the humiliation of teenage years, when a classmate told the class who you had a crush on. Discretion and subtlety are paramount here. All you need is one casual, 'Oh I thought that guy from the other day was interesting,' followed by a nonchalant enquiry and your carefully rehearsed devil-may-care expression. This will set their mind racing, and the irresistible urge we have in us all to set people up will seize control and ensure you bump into each other at the next scheduled event.

TOP TIP

Always keep your ear to the ground to find out who's entered the singles' market. When that hot guy splits up with his girlfriend, you need to be around like a shot. Circumstances change; make sure you move fast when they do.

Alternatively, you can take the reverse tack and contact the guy under the pretence that you're calling for your mutual friend's benefit. The perfect excuse is a surprise party; of course you'll invite him along – the more the merrier. Slightly more sinister is a call of concern. 'Hi, yes, we met the other night, I wanted to speak to you about [mutual friend] because we're really worried about her.'

This is not a particularly healthy start, but it's at least an option, if all else fails.

A better way is to ask your friend to ask him about something specific, as if it's merely a factual enquiry, like,

'Hi, yeah, can you ask that guy from the other night what the name was of that album/hotel/book he was talking about?' Rather than act as middle man in a long conversation, they'll just give you his number and ask you to sort it out yourself.

More subtle still is to fish for him. Let's say you know the guy works as a car mechanic or has a keen interest in pottery, for example. So you send a group email, copying in your mutual friend, asking if anyone knows anyone who can recommend a good garage, or help sell a nice pot you've inherited. Hopefully, they'll take the bait and put you in touch, at which point you feign surprise and go and buy a car/pot quick!

Whichever way you do it, be ruthless about exploiting your friend as a negotiator. If they can't broker the deal, they can perhaps sow some seeds for you and at the very least put you both in contact.

TOP TIP

Always accept every invitation you get. The more random the better. It's a sure way to meet completely new people, and if there's no one you like, you can slip away without anyone noticing.

Other good matches occur through your wider social circle. It's remarkable the number of people who seem to meet their partners at university. This either means they got it on in Freshers'

Week and are still together now (and desperately wishing they'd shagged around a bit more) or they were friends who always quite fancied each other and finally took the plunge one drunken night. But sometimes, it's people they've always vaguely seen about but never really go to know well. When they eventually did, they realised what they'd been missing out on. So it does pay to have a trawl back through your old acquaintances. That nice-enough guy you used to be friends with might have blossomed into a veritable love god.

Lastly, make an effort to meet your friends' friends. It's often the case that when different social circles collide, there are unexpected surprises. Plus, they've already been vouched for by a friend so you know they can't be too bad.

The Office

The expression 'Don't shit on your own doorstep' predates the phenomenon of office romance, yet never could a maxim be more fitting than right here. When a relationship at work goes wrong, it causes an awful lot of trouble, and you will be reminded of some painful truths every single day, while everyone takes great pleasure laughing at you and exchanging instant messages about your every move.

Yet the workplace continues to matchmake more successfully than anywhere else. In fact, 40 per cent of couples meet here. Office romance makes sense because you have both a basic common interest (which may well be a shared loathing of your colleagues) and the opportunity to spend a lot of time together (and get paid for it, yay!). And you never again have to come home and listen to someone droning on about how their day went. So technically it's a hell of a gamble, with the potential of huge loss or reward. But let's face it, we can always do with an urgent career change once in a while.

The best thing about the office is that it offers an incalculable wealth of different flirtation devices. Where else do you have instant messages, Post-it notes, corridor encounters, furtive glances, water-cooler chats, lunches and coffee breaks at your daily disposal? And those emails! The deliberate innuendoes, the vaguest hints and shadows of a suggestion, the glorious ambiguity of a brief sentence or two. You have an arsenal of weapons at your disposal, deploy them keenly and regularly! This is your chance to flirt comprehensively with whoever you like.

Another benefit is that you can interact with your object of desire several times a day for the flimsiest of excuses. Make sure you seek out these encounters. Ask for help with something or orchestrate it so that you work together on a particular project. Sure, there's not much you can do under the glares of the neon lights and your colleagues, but going over proposals over a drink seems reasonable enough.

If these tensions don't bear fruit of their own accord, they will surely find their outlet at the office Christmas party. This behemoth is notorious for good reason. When a year's sexual frustration is suddenly unleashed on a company-wide scale, you can expect unlawful snogging, sweaty embraces, tears and sackings. And, of course, someone vomiting into their own shoes. True, there will be many people to avoid, and you could get in serious trouble but that's the thrill. Do not miss this opportunity to break the ice. None of the usual rules apply so seize your chance while you can.

If you're panicking about the general lack of decent single men at your workplace, remember that guys don't even need to be in your office for you to meet them through work. Think of all the gorgeous people on the outside, whom you meet through 'business dealings'. Of course, it's supposed to be the height of unprofessionalism to sleep with a client (though the opposite is true for prostitutes) but what's wrong with being unprofessional once in a while? You 'borrow' stationery and enjoy the occasional duvet day, why not add a little conflict-of-interest-shagging to the dossier? Besides, your pillow talk might uncover some interesting trade secrets.

How to Pull Personals

Traditionally the reserve of divorcees and university professors, the personals ads have finally emerged from perennial ugly duckling to graceful swan. And nowadays you don't need to be on the point of bequeathing your fortune to a cat sanctuary before you start using them. Personals are everywhere and they're an extremely good idea. Their placement in newspapers and magazines exploits the basic principle about waterholes; always search for the type of man you're after in his natural habitat. So if you're into kite surfing or salsa dancing or some such, a magazine for kite-surfing hunks or snake-hipped salsa enthusiasts is the natural environment to be hunting for the right guy. And if you like intellectuals, well, you're not going to post one in *You Magazine*. With a thoughtfully placed classified, you can ensure that every single man who reads it, let alone responds, will in theory have at least one common interest with you, which is a decent starting point.

The obvious difficulty with personals, though, is that your entry will be featured alongside countless others, and although you are indeed one in a million, you risk melting into the background. Indeed they are so staggeringly similar that most consist of streams of mere acronyms, which makes reading them feel akin to a computer programmer.

So you have '*SF with NSA + GSOH WLTM VGL NS DTE SM 4 TLC.*' What? No RSVP on an SAE at the end? And all that means is: '*Single female with no strings attached and good sense of humour would like to meet very good-looking, non-smoking down-to-earth single male for you-know-what.*'

But isn't that a given? Why else would you post an ad? I mean who doesn't want that? Anyway, if they're so damn keen on saving money on the word count, why not simply write, 'I'M LIKE EVERYONE ELSE.' Ironically, that would work better.

So how do you stick out? Why not try being honest? '*Pissed off with ex, single for two years, this is my last-ditch attempt, do not disappoint me.*' Or '*Have been celibate for so long I think my hymen has resealed. Any help gratefully received in reopening it.*' Well, maybe not quite so honest. Give them a taste of what you really are. Absolutely everyone thinks of themselves as kind, generous, honest, fun, loyal, etc., and while you may be all these things, it doesn't paint a very detailed picture. Whereas if you're a little critical, more of a portrait emerges. This is the model that good drama is based upon; for characters to be interesting they need to be flawed. But why point out my faults, I hear you ask, when I should be concealing them? There are very good reasons for this. Firstly, he'll think yours is the only ad that isn't lying, and secondly, he won't be disappointed when he meets you. So what kind of faults do you reveal? You know that ghastly interview question, 'What would you say is your worst quality?' to which you're supposed to whimper something about being a perfectionist or unable to delegate. Well, it's the same idea. You reveal only the bad qualities you possess which don't create the impression you're unremittingly awful. 'Disorganised, talkative, lazy, brilliant, loud, secretive and saucy,' is a better image of who someone might be than the usual claptrap.

If this all seems too risky though, don't refer to your personality at all. Whereas your character traits tell only so much, cultural references assuredly do. You can tell someone is going to annoy you if they like a really pretentious film or book. So 'huge Kieslowski fan' or 'didn't like Harry Potter' immediately informs you of your compatibility. And if they love something that you love, then you'll get on like a house on fire. A good indicator is comedy. It's super-important that you find the same things funny, so putting a reference to your favourite sitcoms/films is a good lure. If your list of what you like is compatible with theirs, they'll contact you in a flash.

An even cleverer way to screen applicants is a loaded reference. So if you're big on, say, *Anchorman*, a '*Looking for someone who's kind of a big deal*' will register with them and some banter ensues. This does work best for cult classics – the kind of things that attract obsessive fans – and can prompt a degree of bemusement in the uninitiated. But at least they'll be intrigued.

A mistake many ads make is to stipulate what kind of guy they're after. By placing an ad, you're casting your fishing line to single men. Now a keen angler will fit the ideal bait to lure a perfect catch, but won't deliberately make it unattainable to others. If the wrong catch is reeled in, fair enough, you merely let it go and cast again. And you never know, if your basket's still empty by the end of the day you can start being less choosy about what you throw back in (a delightful fish analogy there).

Finally, avoid men who claim they are any of the following: Fun = irritating, Honest = a victim, Sensitive = emotionally vulnerable and needy, Independent = have been single for ages, Passionate = flies into jealous rages, Spiritual = don't go there. Also treat with suspicion anyone who claims they are 'successful'. They are probably just an idiot.

The Internet

It's taken a long time, but finally the taboos surrounding Internet dating have, like the Berlin Wall and many a good soufflé, collapsed. And now we wonder why on earth we didn't embrace it sooner. You have a world of diverse men at your fingertips, who at the very least are computer-literate. You can ruthlessly separate the wheat from the chaff without having to leave your chair. You can laugh at men who blatantly lie about their hobbies (so, he likes ballet, does he?) or have hopelessly vague interests, like 'food, cinema, music and travel'. (Is there anyone who doesn't?) And meanwhile you can post an artfully shot photo that makes you look incredible and create a profile that portrays you as the best catch in the entire world (wide web). The downfall is that eventually meeting them can be a let-down, but hey-ho there are so many more on the list. Hopefully though, the email banter will have road-tested whether you're going to get on, and his looks, well, you'd never be so shallow as to judge someone on his looks, would you?

Various points of Internet dating etiquette are that it's OK to have countless men on the go in the cyber world at the same time before you settle on one, you can flirt with people even if you don't fancy them, and you don't have to worry about upsetting people when you reject them because it's simply the rules of the game. You can also put your profile on every single site without losing face, you can come off and on the dating scene at the touch of a button and you can be on the pull 24/7. True, it is embarrassing when a site's search criteria matches you with someone you already know and don't fancy, but it's hardly legally binding.

Successfully hooking nice guys on the Internet is a skill, which can borrow heavily from the trail that personals have blazed for aeons. You now know the tricks of writing a good profile, but the Internet puts one more key resource at your disposal: your picture. When you're posting a picture of yourself online, don't use one of you standing with a friend, even it's your most flattering shot. It will look like you don't have a better one and they will invariably think you're the other girl. A party shot is usually a good option, because you're dressed up and smiling. But should you use a posed one or an action shot? This is often a choice between looking decent but vain or looking fun but a bit ropey. Go for the posed one. Certainly don't use the webcam on your computer. That makes anyone look like a serial killer.

Brilliantly, the Internet also provides a trail of unwitting clues to the men you're spying on. If they've posted on a dating site, they'll have a presence elsewhere which you can track down to find out more about them. Discussion forums, virtual worlds, social networking sites, file sharing: anything can reveal more of their character, and more effectively than the classic Google search.

User names, for example, are a brilliant indicator of what people are truly like. If he's called KrollTheAvenger or WildStallionLover, you know that he's a 14-year-old boy with bumfluff and box of Kleenex by his side. If there's a number after his name, such as jedimaster4521 or theone-andonly29063, it suggests he's not exactly one in a million. Promising user names are ones with a degree of wit or which are self-deprecating somehow. Same with avatars. People who genuinely try to make their avatars look attractive or muscular are clearly trying to conceal something dubious. Surely the Internet is the one place you can run around to your heart's content looking like shit. Or better still, like a little squirrel. Or a fat purple manatee. Email addresses are a good source of info too. A work address says they're strictly above board – no monkey business – and gives an idea of what they do for a living, same

TOP TIP

Should you ever adopt a persona in order to pull? Let's be honest, this can be highly successful, but it does prove quite tricky in the long run. Perhaps fine-tuning your personality is best. Like with your CV, you should miss off the disasters and trumpet the triumphs.

with a vanilla address which just has their name, and sometimes people helpfully include their age as in bensmith1977@howtopull.com. I suppose they might lie though.

Finding someone on the Internet doesn't necessarily need to occur on a dating site. Forums are a good way to get to know someone via the back door. Extremely tight communities build up super-fast, get to know each other in an unusually short space of time and 'talk' all hours of the day and night, all under the safety umbrella of a shared interest. True, people's Internet personae do not necessarily tally with the real thing, but it's a good way of road-testing them.

TOP TIP

If you believe in star signs, keep that a closely guarded secret. Never reveal that it affects your judgements. In particular, do not ask a guy his star sign. He will suspect you are a witch.

Lastly, and in the general spirit of fun, a warning. In the same way that for superheroes great power comes with great responsibility, on the Internet great anonymity comes with great opportunities for sweaty sex pests. I'm sure you've been astounded on a few occasions when an apparently amiable exchange suddenly became X-rated. Maybe you didn't notice when he started enquiring about what you were wearing, thinking 'Oh, how sweet, he doesn't want me to catch my death of cold.' Yup, there's a universe of drooling perverts out there and the Internet has released them from the bonds of convention. So be vigilant and the moment something seems peculiar, start acting like a psycho and it will usually scare them off.

Speed Dating

Purists might argue that speed dating is symptomatic of a society increasingly deriving its kicks from quick fixes, and they're mostly right, but, boy, is this an efficient way to road-test men. First impressions are everything, and so they should be because this approach is based upon the indefinable commodity of whether you 'click'. You'll have to pay for the privilege, but it's worth it for its ruthless pragmatism. And while three minutes might seem like too little time to get to know someone, you'll be grateful for its brevity when you're sitting opposite a complete idiot. At the end, you have the option to tick boxes for each guy to say whether you like them or not. The jury's out on whether a buckshot approach pays off (where you tick absolutely everyone and see who comes back) but it's always nice to know you're in demand. Go with a friend and give it a try.

A funny thing about speed dating though is that half of the extremely brief conversation is spent convincing each other that you don't normally do this and that you just came along for a laugh. Next time someone starts protesting too much, say, 'For a laugh? Really? I'm here to find a husband.' That'll teach them to apply the brakes before they've even started moving. Moreover, both parties are reluctant to talk about themselves because they want to know about one another. It's quite telling what details they do reveal, because in such a short space of time, a great deal of unsubtle showing off is employed. Alarm bells should go off if he describes himself as an 'entrepreneur', discusses salary, mentions his car, makes reference to any sporting achievement like the Iron Man challenge, or lets slip his tireless marathon runs for orphans, etc. And beware of pre-prepared lines. When someone asks you, 'If you were an animal what would you be?' they've either been watching reruns of *Blind Date* or their normal conversation stinks.

TOP TIP

If you're getting on with someone amazingly and feel really ballsy, you can always suggest that you both abandon the production line mid-flow and go and have a drink together. That would be quite impressive.

Weddings

We go to weddings so we can share the moment of happiness of someone special and celebrate their endless love with joyous music and laughter. But a large part of going to a wedding is because we want to pull. And most people feel legally entitled to do so at a wedding.

Certainly the prospects are good: love is in the air so everyone should be in the mood, hopefully all the single people have been put next to each other at the wedding breakfast (though it's utterly baffling why some hosts still fail to see to this), and everyone has scrubbed up nicely. True, elderly relatives may be present and you will undoubtedly have to field endless questions about the inconsequential details of your busy life, but ignore them and you're laughing. For this is the mother of opportunities to pull.

Now, the key to pulling well at a wedding is to spot your prey early. And I mean indecently early. A real pro should have chosen their target before the bride has even turned up. So once you've taken your seat, take a long look around and start processing information fast. Sweep the room like an MI5 agent at a terrorist convention. And rest assured that for once you're actually allowed to gawp shamelessly at people. Indeed, it's actively encouraged. If you do, however, get embarrassed, wave at someone random; they're bound to assume they know you and wave back.

So what are the hallmarks of a good catch here? He's not the man clutching the toddler, or the one wearing the ceremonial robes. You might secretly wish he were the man at the altar, but stop that right away; you had your chance, you're not helping matters. Single men should stick out like a sore thumb here, because generally speaking, if they're going out with anyone of any permanence, she'll be beside him, squeezing his hand oh-so-tightly as she dreamily conjures up a more securely committed future for them both.

No, the single men are conspicuous by their solitude. Try as they might to blend in (and they won't), they're scattered everywhere, plain as day. In pairs, tagging on to couples, prowling the aisles with a manufactured air of efficiency, lurking on their own at the back like besuited rebels on a school bus. It won't take long for them to clock you either. Hold their gaze, if you can, and continue your ruthless search, until your view is blocked by the billowy mass that is the bride. Now smile graciously and enjoy the show.

By this point, your perusal may have engendered a sense of panic of the kind that goes 'For ****'s sake, I've spent sixty quid on this hat and there's no one even half-decent here,' but fret not. The beauty of a wedding is that new people continually emerge from the woodwork. Be patient and they will appear.

Seconds after the ceremony is over, you're in the best possible time to strike, so look sharp – you must make initial contact here, however brief, to save you heaps of time and trouble later. As people mill around cooing over the happy couple and waiting for the photos to be taken, there's a widely observed truce that allows you to chat to anyone standing near you without arousing suspicion. You can turn to total strangers at this point and mutter any number of accepted wedding phrases. 'Wasn't that lovely?' 'Don't they look happy?' 'Didn't the mother look frumpy in her dress!' And it's always rather nice, this uncharacteristic bonding fest, so savour every moment of it and – again I must stress – move fast. Amble around until you can station yourself next to someone you do like and engineer a brief exchange. Start with a conventional platitude as an ice-breaker, then follow with whatever comes naturally. The conversation may be brief, but that doesn't matter in the least. The whole point is to whet the appetite, to plant the seeds that will be watered later on. Indeed you might deliberately endeavour to keep it short, the briefer the better, and as soon as you have his interest, break it off and go and talk to someone you know well. He will resolve to catch you later.

I cannot stress the importance of this initial dalliance. The pulling won't start till after the meal, but then you have every reason to bump into him with a 'hello again' and jokey comparisons of how you're enjoying yourselves. This is so much easier than a 'cold' approach later, a 'Hello, I don't believe we've met.' The ready-established familiarity will make the conversation run more smoothly and he'll subconsciously feel he already knows you. Of course it's all heavily orchestrated, but it will have the semblance of spontaneity and that, my friends, is the essence of pulling.

The drinks part of the reception is a tricky one, because you probably want to talk to the people you know. Indeed, you won't endear yourself to your friends if you scrupulously avoid them in your search for romantic gratification. Normally, I would say screw the friends and get pulling, but you're at a wedding so there's time for both. The worst mistake, though, is to get trapped in the tedium of an unwanted conversation. Old people love chatting to the youngsters and at wedding receptions they reckon they've got you cornered. Sure, it's the decent thing to do, to infuse them with some of your youthful energy and zest for life, but you're not Mother Teresa, so ditch them as soon as you can. They'll be resigned to this. Get back into the fray, subtly manoeuvring your position in the room with each encounter so you get ever closer to that cool-looking guy.

TOP TIP

If none of the guests take your fancy, don't rule out the staff. Waiters, barmen, DJs, photographers (hey, he might be a war journalist during the week!). Not sure if that includes the cab driver on the way home though.

TOP TIP

Be mindful of the best man. He believes there's some ancient bylaw entitling him to pull whomsoever he chooses. If he does kiss you, there's no guarantee he will stop there; he may well slip away to raise his tally. Particularly if he reckons you won't put out.

TOP TIP

If you don't know anyone, make friends with other randoms immediately. They can introduce you to others and provide valuable wingman duties. And by the way, don't ever try and catch the bouquet. It just makes you look desperate.

At dinner, you need to get to your table before anyone else and scout out who you've been seated next to. More often than not, you'll be sat next to some tiresome gimp who is far from ideal. Or more probably between a married couple. Now you face the moral dilemma of our age: is it acceptable to change the seating plan? Well, I reckon if the hosts have been cack-handed enough to overlook a decent matchmaking table plan – surely the most basic of priorities – then you must take the law into your own hands. Plonk yourself next to the best option and await their arrival.

After dinner you merely reap the benefits of the good work you've done before by bumping into the man you like by the bar or on the dance floor or joining his table. Piece of cake.

Random Encounters

You're sitting opposite a guy on the train; he's incredibly cute but you just can't force yourself to talk to him. Not an uncommon problem and not just restricted to trains. You'll no doubt rationalise that he's probably not single or remotely interesting, or that he'll cut you down the moment you open your mouth. Heck, the last time someone talked to you on the train, he smelt of wee and claimed the government had him under surveillance. But this is the prime time to meet a stranger. Things clearly aren't happening with the people you know, so why not take a stab in the dark? It's surely situations like this that throw up all sorts of surprise twists, such as stalking, harassment, murder…sorry, I mean glorious, unexpected romance. Yes, the risks are high but there's something insanely romantic about chancing upon someone out of the blue, as if you've clutched each other from the sea of souls. Admit it, you've read those slightly vulgar stories in trashy magazines where a chance encounter led to someone being swept off their feet. You know, the ones which end with, 'Now the man of my dreams is marrying me, with our two beautiful children as bridesmaids.' You probably sighed with contentment before turning the page to laugh at someone whose weight had ballooned. And this is probably how the happy couple of the story met. Or on a plane or in a supermarket, park, gym, cinema queue, gallery, ice rink, beach or even a church/ temple/ synagogue. (I would include mosques but women are segregated, so not much luck there.)

So how do you make your move when you see him? The shared location provides everything you need. You're both travelling/ walking the dog/ shopping/ queuing/ praying so there's every excuse to talk about it. The trick is seamlessly moving on to a more interesting subject without it seeming contrived. Chances are, whatever you say, he's bound to agree with you and will add something to take it in another direction. A gag is guaranteed to do this. If you joke about something, particularly about how shit something is, a man will jump at the challenge of bouncing back with a retort. Once you're laughing, you're away.

It's always worth a go. You'll kick yourself if you don't muster up the courage. And there are so many get-out clauses if it goes wrong. If you're stuck next to them for an extended duration – on the train for example – you can listen to music, carefully study the emergency information or play Tetris on your mobile. Or try making a prolonged animal noise and watch him avoid you like the plague. In all other cases, just walk away. You were just being friendly.

A subset of the Random Encounter is a business transaction. The waiter who's been giving you the eye all meal, the sales assistant who flirted with you outrageously, even the doctor who takes extra-special care of you. Surely, you shouldn't? Of course you should. That's what they're there for. Sure, it's a bit tricky to change gear from sales patter to friendly chatter. You can't move that smoothly from 'Is service included?' to 'Are you single?' (Though why not, I'm not sure.) However, all these occasions offer you the opportunity to write down your number and give it to them. This carries with it obvious risks, as you may find yourself changing your mind immediately afterwards, but hey ho.

And what happens if it's you doing the serving? Propositioning customers/ patients/ clients is invariably frowned upon in most establishments. But he's hardly likely to complain, is he? Just make sure you don't get caught. Or if you don't want to risk it, a suggestive variation of your usual sales patter should get the message home.

TOP TIP
Wearing headphones in public only makes you less approachable. Perhaps that's the whole point.

We can't ignore the fact that all of these random encounters require one of you to approach the other entirely out of the blue and make conversation, which requires nerves of steel. You may not have them – very few do – but this is a time where bluffing will pay off. If you don't hit it off you may never see them again.

Your Best Friend

What do you do if you've fallen for your best friend? Start feeling very, very anxious is the honest answer because this is a genuinely tricky situation. The stakes don't get any higher, since you stand to either gain everything or lose it all. But played well, this could be the greatest thing that ever happens to you.

Just Friends Syndrome starts imperceptibly enough. You spend more and more time together but it's fine because he's got a girlfriend or you don't fancy each other or it happened years ago and is so behind you both. You arrive and leave as a couple but no one suspects anything, least of all you. Strangers ask if you're together and you both laugh, as if, yeah, right, like that's going to happen. You acknowledge that he's the greatest guy in the whole world but the chemistry is just not there. Then one day it hits you. 'Holy shit! I'm completely in love with him.'

And it's not that you simply fancy him; you're utterly besotted in the blink of an eye. So what do you do? Well, you avoid him of course.

This moment of realisation is fraught with anxiety and is seldom a happy one. Because you fear the worst, you present yourself with a number of unfavourable 'what if's. What if he doesn't like me? What if I mess this up? What if we go out and it's a disaster? The one 'what if' you don't ask yourself is, 'But what if we don't get together and have to spend the rest of our lives apart?' If you've fallen in love with your best friend, it's too late to rationalise. You need to just calm down and work out the best way to bring it to a happy conclusion. Only you understand the dynamics of your friendship and the best means of ultra-sensitive diplomacy required to seal this deal. It's a fair bet, though, that a tearful confession won't work. The best course of action is to increase the pace until you 'accidentally' kiss and then gauge their reaction. Either way, good luck and proceed with caution.

Valentine's Day

Valentine's Day has to be the best thing in the world. Traditionally a day of utter dread for single people (when else does your heart fill with joy when the postman arrives?), Valentine's is in fact a golden ticket to seize the day. Hey, there's even a saint backing you up on this one. Yes, it's a bit tacky, yes, it's a commercial scam, yes, it makes couples seem even smugger, but sod it: this day you're positively encouraged to blow your cover. So why not go to town on this one? Don't just send one card; send one to every single person you've ever vaguely liked the look of. Look people up who you haven't seen for years and send them one. They won't be signed so you can always deny everything and wriggle away if need be, but they could be laced with clues that can be traced back straight to you, if that is your aim. Ultimately you want this person to fancy you; this goes a good way to planting that thought if it's not already there.

If you're having dinner with someone that night, make sure you go somewhere low key. It can be really awkward when the restaurant offers a compulsory, exorbitant Valentine's Day menu. It's bad enough having to pay more than double for a pretty average meal, but worse still when a romantic atmosphere is rammed forcefully down your neck. There's the themed food like 'heart of artichoke', 'love soup' and 'prawn star', there's the inappropriate encouragements from waiters, and there's the mutual loathing of other diners, all scrutinising to see who is having the most romantic time. Heaven forbid there might be an amateur musician to serenade you or an illegal immigrant hawking a bucket of roses and trying to make you feel guilty. Yes, it's truly amazing how off kilter the commercialist view of romance invariably proves. Romance, it seems, cannot be bought.

If you're not booked for dinner, keep your options open for the evening. Don't do anything that might not result in pulling the person you want to. If someone you don't really fancy asks you out for dinner, say no. If you don't know anyone you do fancy, go somewhere you could find someone. Go out for a drink on your own if you must because you can fully guarantee tonight that everyone who is single will be looking for love. Yes, for Valentine's Day, you need to be ruthless. Resist the temptation to denounce the whole affair and eschew a night out. Even if you claim you don't believe in it (come off it), even if you have found it mildly degrading in the past, console yourself that you will be more depressed if you stay at home.

Members of the Family

Though somewhat frowned upon and technically illegal in this country, marrying into your own family has an enthusiastic following among deeply religious communities. There are advantages though: you have nice in-laws, not too many guests at the wedding, your children will be 'special,' and, er, what am I saying? Don't even consider it. Seriously. Or your eyebrows will conjoin and your teeth will fall out. Fact!

Movie kisses that nearly didn't happen 2: *Pretty Woman*

Let's not beat around the bush: Julia Roberts plays a sex worker. Whereas a considerable proportion of men will shag one on business trips, they don't want to go out with one. Correction: they don't want to be seen to go out with one but they nevertheless harbour a secret desire to rescue them, as illustrated by Richard Gere. That is why you can excuse drunkards on stag nights bleating to the topless girl grinding her pudenda into his thigh, 'You're too good for this, I can rescue you from this sordid world (can I touch them yet?)' Men, however, seldom do rescue them. They like the idea of the damsel in distress, particularly if she's guaranteed to be filthy in bed. But with a hooker comes a past, and guys like to think that, while you're well experienced, you haven't shagged everything that moves. This, I believe, sums up the virgin/whore complex. They expect the result without its necessary endeavours. So Roberts is at a disadvantage from the start.

Another disadvantage is her peculiar unworldliness. *Pretty Woman* is essentially the *Pygmalion* story, or *My Fair Lady*, if you prefer. Rich but arrogant man meets lovely but uncultured girl and sets about improving her, but she in fact ends up improving him. Gere seems to find her poor manners delightfully charming, when in reality they would be quite annoying. True, she's a breath of fresh air in his social circle where falseness and pretentiousness abound, but then there's hardly much competition: his friends are horrendous. But, to be frank, her endearingly honest naivety just begins to grate after a while. Yes, she's a fish out of water, but she's hardly Crocodile Dundee. You'd expect her to vaguely know how to behave. Get a grip, Roberts!

A particularly onerous example of her naivety is when she tearfully reveals that she has always dreamt of being swept off her feet by a knight in shining armour atop a white horse. I mean, give me a break. You can almost hear Gere groan inwardly. Men resent romantic concepts of their chivalrous role in the same way girls objects to men's attempts to make them behave like porn stars. Because it's a film, he does in fact turn up as the dashing knight (complete with umbrella), but that is because he's rich enough to afford it. Most men can't. The best we can do is sweep you off your feet in a Vauxhall Corsa, bringing with us a bunch of garage flowers. We can't stand the pressure, so stop dreaming of Prince Charming. You're not Cinderella.

I've been bit harsh here, so I should admit that Julia Roberts's girlishness does have its charms. Remember the scene where she reaches for the jewellery box and it snaps shut on her fingers. You probably know this was an accident during filming, but they decided to keep it in the film (if you look closely you can see her look round for the director). The reason this sequence works so well is because Roberts exudes an infectious cheer and an uncynical lust for life. You'd expect that after years on her back, she'd be jaded but yet she still has this youthful exuberance.

A mistake she also cannot be blamed for is her dress sense. A prostitute panders to the basest male fantasies, but thigh-high boots? Are you serious? Please spare us. And the wig? What the hell is that about? Come on, wardrobe department.

The best thing Julia Roberts does is to resist his charms. She is the only girl not trying to 'land' him, and that is what makes her so attractive to him. Although he is paying for her, she cannot be bought. She has strong morals and refuses to compromise them. This is what Richard Gere falls for. She's the only person he cannot manipulate.

Ultimately, *Pretty Woman* is the most romantic tale of redemption. Together, two lost souls are able to find each other and themselves. here is a good place to remind you that men who have had unprotected intercourse with a sex worker have a high incidence of chlamydia, thrush, gonorrhoea and anal warts.

PART THREE

Dating him

Setting the Date

You're going on a date. This is good news. But there is little time to rejoice and much work to be done. Two important decisions immediately present themselves: when and where. Both are of equal importance. And both are key to a great date. Hopefully the kind of man you're after will allow you some say in the matter so push for your agenda; it will pay off.

We'll start with *when*. Days of the week have traditionally been an unused weapon in the diverse arsenal of pulling tactics. Few bother to arrange dates on unconventional

TOP TIP

Being late for a rendezvous is accepted and expected; it's a mark of style and an indication that you're independent. But there are some things you cannot be late for: surprise parties, firework displays, planes, your own wedding and films that he's really excited about. Be late for these and understandably he will go apeshit.

days. But dates don't necessarily have to conform to the Thursday–Saturday window. Particularly as that's when all the best television is on.

So, Sunday then? Who'd go on a date on Sunday evening? You would if you had any sense. Think about it. You're always free (the cinema can wait), it feels a bit naughty because there's work the next day and you can spend all week looking forward to it without spoiling your busy weekend plans. Or Wednesday? Beautifully poised in the middle of the week, who'd pick on innocent little Wednesday? And if things go according to plan on the Wednesday it's not too forward to suggest meeting up on the Sunday again. Two for one! Woo hoo!

Whatever day you choose, fixing it presents a golden opportunity for you to play games. Now, lovers who 'play games' soon get a bad name for themselves, but this is a harmless game and plays a vital role. Say he rings you and suggests Friday night. Do you accept and reveal that you didn't have any plans for the busiest night of the week? Like, hello, loser alert! Of course you don't. You turn him down and suggest another. The same applies for any day he suggests in fact. Even boring, unsexy Monday. 'Can't do it, sadly,' you say. (Subtext: I'm so damn popular that you better work hard for me, boy!) And don't say what you're doing, simply purr, 'I'm out that night.' Hell, you might be at the chiropodist's having your bunions surgically removed, but for all he knows you're out clubbing with trendy people.

TOP TIP

Do not reveal that you have a routine. If you have to turn down a date by saying, 'On Mondays I have book club,' he will think, 'Alas, I'll only ever be able to see her six days a week.'

All this has to be handled delicately though because he'll be looking for the slightest hint that you're not keen. When you do turn down one day, be sure to sound enthusiastic about an alternative. Everyone understands the shorthand of 'This week's a bit of a nightmare', or 'Let's try and sort something another time.' Be sure that he doesn't think you're fobbing him off.

Perversely, it's sod's law that you'll meet someone nice right before you enter an intensely busy period, like exams, a work project or a family crisis. Almost as if the stars have conspired to give a glimpse of happiness only to snatch it away again. And though you would love to go on a date with him, it's not always possible. It's quite hard to convince someone that you're interested when you can't fit them in for a fortnight. You feel like saying, 'I know we don't know each other but *please* be patient and wait for me.' Yikes – not entirely convincing. But do you risk meeting up in the middle of your crisis and not being on form?

Only you can make this painful choice.

You've set the day, now for the time. The earlier, the better. If it's at the weekend, go for 7 p.m.; that way you have a whole glorious evening ahead of you, or alternatively the possibility of another engagement conveniently scheduled for later on if the going gets tough. If it's during the week, go either early or late, not in the middle. Most people finish work and don't want to have to wait around getting nervous before the big event when both parties could easily have met already. Implicit in all this is that if a drink goes well, it will meander smoothly into dinner, which is probably what you both want. Meeting early certainly gives you options.

TOP TIP

Do not pretend you don't know who's calling when you've obviously already got his number programmed into your mobile phone. Everyone sees through this foolish ploy.

The *where* is harder to control, as a man will have put a lot of thought into this if he likes you and it's quite tricky to veto his venue simply on the grounds that it's crap. Pre-empting him early on with the suggestion of a place that you've heard is great and have always wanted to go to will work a treat though. He'll somehow feel considerate for agreeing to it and congratulate himself for choosing a place you'll like, while not being threatened that it's your territory, since you've never been there. (Delicate thing, the male ego.)

Another unusual tactic might be to railroad him outright. When he asks you if you might be willing, um, to er, possibly go out for a drink maybe sometime, say something like, 'Sure, meet me next Tuesday at seven in Café Blanc,' then walk off/ hang up. It will scare the crap out of him and he'll undoubtedly agree and cancel whatever he had planned. He'll also think you're super-confident and sexy. (Warning: this may backfire.)

Considerations for a good venue, therefore, are: making sure you won't bump into anyone you know – they will invariably try to make conversation at the wrong moment. Not telling your friends where you're going (this applies mainly to the man because his friends most likely will turn up to snigger). Trying to pick somewhere far from your house as the 'walk-you-home' moment is awkward at best and downright scary the rest of the time. Finding somewhere which exudes the image of the sort of person you are, i.e., not a trashy sports bar or anodyne pub chain.

TOP TIP

Do not read your horoscope before you go on a date. It will only make you screw up.

REAL-LIFE DATE

'We'd planned our first date weeks in advance but when it came up, she had a hospital appointment rescheduled to that morning for a minor operation. I suggested we postpone but she was damned if we were going to miss out on our long-awaited evening together. Anyway, when we met, she looked really pale and spaced out and kept apologising for everything. We had a drink and after a couple of sips, she slumped to the floor and bumped her head. Turned out she hadn't eaten for 24 hours. She wasn't really hurt, but I suggested taking her home. She told me she was fine, I gave her some water, but she did exactly the same thing again, except this time she was sick on the chair leg. I took her to hospital and she stayed there for 48 hours. But I pulled her a week later. Ha!'

The Bar Date

'Meeting for a drink' is brilliantly vague and could lead to all sorts of things. Yes, you're in for a night bursting with potential. Your first good move is to get there before him. Military commanders stress the importance of gaining the higher ground in conflict, so it is with the date. If you turn up after him you'll look slightly uncool scanning the venue for your date – best leave this to him. Turning up early means you can suss out the environment, choose where to sit and, best of all, collect yourself. When he arrives you'll be cool, calm and collected, rather than flustered and lightly perspiring.

So you're there, all is well; the short wait is on. At this point you may be tempted to play with your mobile phone. Don't. Yes, you do have reception, no, that random text can wait, no, he hasn't rung to cancel. You've surely sniggered once at someone alone in a bar, who tried to make it clear that they were not a lonely loser by repeatedly looking at their watch/mobile phone and sighing exaggeratedly. Avoid making the same mistake. Besides if he turns up and you're looking at it, he'll think you're panicking about being stood up. Contrived though it might seem, an excellent solution is to read something (not the list of bar snacks, however tempting) because it gives the impression you're not too fussed, always a good thing. And it also gives a handy prop for emergencies. Your choice of reading matter can deliberately impress (a well-thumbed copy of Proust/ *Razzle*/ *Bravo Two Zero*, for example) or better yet serve as a back-up if the chat falters. 'Yes, I've just been reading about global warming – isn't it terrible!' or some such, if things get desperate.

Choosing a drink can also be a canny means of impressing someone. There's no sweeter sound to a guy at this point than you saying, 'Shall we just share a bottle of wine?' It means you're guaranteed to be there for an hour or so, you're up for a laugh, not too worried about getting tipsy and it hopefully steps up the intimacy levels. It also gives him the opportunity to try and show off with the wine list. (NB: Be heartened if he struggles to choose a wine, or goes for one from the film *Sideways*, as nice guys usually know nothing about wine.)

Of course you'll order what you feel like, but drinks can give off unintentional vibes. Spritzers are for WAGs, pints are either unbelievably sexy/bit of a turn-off depending on your date's view and alcopops are beneath contempt. Champagne is extremely tricky territory; if you opt for some it will irritate him, no matter how much he likes

TOP TIP

Never admit to a man that you have looked him up on the Internet. True, he will have done his own research on you, but neither should let it slip. What you can do is steer the conversation on to territory you know applies to him.

TOP TIP

When you're on a date, set the alarm on your mobile for halfway through proceedings and change its ringtone to sound like a text message. Then, when the 'text' arrives, look annoyed that you're being disturbed and ignore it. That way he'll think you're popular and digging his company.

you, because at this stage he'll think he's paying. And if he suggests some, it means he's flashing cash in a pathetic attempt to schmooze you and is probably a tosser. Either way, save the bubbles for a special occasion – like your anniversary!

So what happens after the first drink? You probably know this, but guys often judge how much a girl likes him by how many drinks she has on the date. So when he offers you a second/ third drink, your acceptance or refusal is a clear signal of whether you're interested or not. Now this is by no means a clarion call for binge drinking; it doesn't even mean the drinks have to be alcoholic – otherwise people of a religious disposition (God bless 'em) and teetotallers would be doomed – it's just that the offer of another drink is a search for reassurance. Agreeing to another one is a subtle affirmation you still fancy him. Therefore refusing another is often a nice way to make them back off without having to say so. And men, though clumsy fools, will invariably pick up on this. So if you think the guy's a creep, order one mineral water, drink it quickly and he'll get the message.

TOP TIP

If you spend too much time in the loos on a date, he will assume you're texting friends to request back-up. You may well be. Reassure him if you haven't.

REAL-LIFE DATE

'I was chatting to this really cool girl in a bar, when this guy butted in and started telling us how much travelling he'd done and how "humbled" he felt by the experience. He went on and on about places we'd never been to, talked about their "energy" and other crap like that, marvelled at the dawn light on Machu Picchu and so on. Nightmare. Eventually, the girl told him she was so inspired that she was off this minute to the travel agents', grabbed my hand and we ran out. It was so ballsy – I thought she was great. Should have seen the look on his face. "Humbled" indeed.'

The Restaurant Date

The restaurant date exudes the classic vision of romance. Having dinner out with anyone is a treat, even with your family, so dining with someone you fancy is a pleasure overload. You get to eat by candlelight without it seeming cheesy, the staff are under orders to be nice to you, you can have a starter, main *and* dessert, heck, you even get those free mints at the end (but don't touch them – they're covered in piss, don't you know!). In fact a restaurant date is so goddamn near perfect that there must surely be no need for tips and strategy. Yet, as ever, there are still a few tricks you can have up your sleeve.

★

CHILLING STATISTIC

33% of scientists expect you to go Dutch on the first date

Great news then. Men feel comforted by the ability to pay for your meal. Best order a nice starter.

Whatever you do, share a starter. Or better still, a dessert. In fact, always go for the dessert. It's extremely intimate, quite flirty, you can fight over the last scraps (always a winner) and you don't have to stuff your face too much. And make sure you both have a bit of each other's main course. Dipping your fork into someone's personal space will set anyone's blood racing. The only shortcoming of this is if your food is so good that it will piss you off to have to give any away.

TOP TIP

Instead of sitting opposite each other, engineer it so you're side by side, preferably on a banquette. For some reason you can flirt more this way and maybe snatch a cheeky smooch.

REAL-LIFE DATE

'A rather lovely girl and I were having a real laugh over dinner challenging each other to see who could eat the spiciest food. She upped the stakes by downing a neat mouthful of Tabasco, then started crying and dry-heaving over her plate. I felt really bad for her and held her hair back as she repeatedly spat into an ashtray. I reckoned she must have liked me a lot to pull a stunt like that. Thought it was quite sweet. We're now married but avoid spicy food, as you can imagine.'

Another way to gain immediate favour is ordering the water. You will no doubt have noticed how waiting staff in posh restaurants increasingly try and emotionally blackmail you into splashing out on water. The sneering 'Still or sparkling?' with its distinct lack of a third option makes most of us suckers bite the bullet and buy some overpriced, kooky-shaped bottle. Men only agree to this to avoid looking like a cheapskate. But if you give the waiter a steely-eyed look and reply, 'Tap,' your grateful paramour will breathe a sigh of relief and think you're admirably unfussy. But then again, if you feel like being spoilt, sod it and order both.

TOP TIP

Demeaning though it may be, it pays to have a couple of amazing facts up your sleeve in case conversation is not running smoothly. This is not the same as having a pre-prepared take on a hot topic, like world poverty or the GI diet.

Contrary to popular opinion, if a guy pays for dinner, he does not expect anything in return. He knows this is no transaction. He's not thinking, 'She'll shag me if I throw in some coffee and cheese.' He might reasonably hope for a snog if it's gone well, but that, like the tip, is at your discretion.

TOP TIP

Do laugh at his jokes if you can bear to. This guy is shitting himself; desperately trying to make you laugh, so throw him a lifeline once in a while. Do not laugh too much though. He will grow tired of the non-challenge and get lazy.

REAL-LIFE DATE

'I quite fancied this girl, so I took her out for dinner, where she insisted on ordering every aphrodisiac available on the menu. She had everything: champagne, oysters, asparagus, potatoes, chocolate, strawberries... If there'd been tiger penis, she'd have had that too! And all the time she kept winking and smiling suggestively, like she was going to shag my brains out. When the bill arrived, it was so extortionate that my card was declined. She didn't have a cent so I had to go all the way home to fetch another card, which took an hour and a half, by which time she'd left. God knows what happened to her when those aphrodisiacs kicked in.'

The Diversion Date

The diversion date is when you invite a guy to go and see something with you, without officially acknowledging it's a date. Relatively easy to set up, it maintains an implicit I'm-not-too-keen quality about it, which suggests you would be going anyway and just thought they might like it too. Basically, it exudes control. So when you ring to say 'there's this great exhibition of German Expressionism/ all-male performance of *Romeo and Juliet*/ silent movie retrospective with live jazz accompaniment/ modern-dance interpretation of the Koran and I think you'd like it,' you are fulfilling several key criteria. You are exhibiting a steely independence, perhaps the most important on your checklist of good impressions to give, a passion, which is a reliably attractive quality, and the fact that you are thinking about them – flattery will get you everywhere. Now the one drawback is that you may propose something that is deeply unpalatable (like all of the above), and here the danger of coming across as pretentious should be paramount in your mind. Human nature is such that with most cultural reference, a certain amount of obfuscation occurs. We've all done it. Someone asks you what music you're listening to at the moment, but you don't say, 'Well actually I've been dancing round my bedroom to the *Greatest Hits of Right Said Fred*,' no your hypothalamus switches to overdrive and you drone on about some MySpace wannabe you're meant to like. So pick something you'll both want to go to, not something you feel you ought to go to.

TOP TIP
Be self-deprecating once for charm. Twice begins to irk.

Gigs are great because you're guaranteed three things: a euphoric finale (which will naturally propel you into his loving arms) a slow number (which will do much the same thing) and some form of disagreement with a fellow concert-goer (once again, into his arms). The risk is with the music itself, so check their music tastes well in advance.

REAL-LIFE DATE

'I went to a festival with a new girlfriend. First day our tent gets nicked – completely disappeared. Only thing left was a pair of socks, and they weren't even ours. I had a major malfunction but she was really cool about it, even though she'd lost a lot of nice clothes and stuff. We decided to just keep partying through anyway and not sleep. Had a wicked night. It really brought us together. We kept the socks as a souvenir.'

Comedy shows are good for dates too. They're informal, so you can sort of chat and you laugh together, which, like crying, is a peculiarly intimate experience. Two dangers though: a brilliant routine might make you fall for the comedian instead, or you might be the unlucky buggers who get picked on throughout the performance. It's hard to feel sexy when you've had your appearance and hometown ridiculed all night.

Ah, the art gallery. How many young lovers have ambled wide-eyed and enthusiastic through this nation's exhibitions, never to admit to each other that they couldn't have given a shit about what was on display? We love to love art. But we don't really like it. The problem with these places is that they exude an inescapable air of solemnity. This can easily be confused with boredom. And though you may have an interest, you're unlikely to have 'fun' as it is commonly understood. Those private views and gallery launches are good though. If you're not 'lucky' enough to be invited, you should be cunning enough to gatecrash. If you do pass one by, always slip in. There's free booze, you can snigger at the artworks and gawp incredulously at the pretentious people refusing to smile. Why not ask the DJ (yes seriously, some of these wank-fests use decks to try and appropriate some 'cool') for grossly inappropriate songs like 'Candle in the Wind' or 'Itsy Bitsy Teeny Weeny Yellow Polka Dot Bikini'? Another advantage is that it won't take long before one of you breaks and declares, 'Screw this shit, let's go,' cue much drinking and piss-taking in another, better venue.

At the cinema, don't go to a film that you really, really want to see or that's one of your favourites. You will respond poorly, even irritably to any interruptions or worse, incessantly rant, 'Oh my God, this next bit is so cool.' Guys are the worst about this so make sure you don't see one of his. Do people still go to any old crappy film so they can sit in the back row and snog away to their heart's content? It's a cliché, so it must be true. But I'm betting you haven't done it for a while. The reason young teenagers do it is that for them getting a snog overshadows all other concerns on this planet, and, while it may sometimes feel that way to you, you're a grown girl now, so at least pretend you're interested in the film.

OK, so you may not be after a love bite, but you still want some affection during the film. That means you're left with a few tried and tested options. The horror film is a classic. It's so scary, ghastly, terrifying, so horrifically real, the only escape is…to seek shelter in the arms of your lover and protector. This is what guys are counting on. Try not to disappoint him; just scream if you want to go further. Sadly the reverse isn't true; the more a guy whimpers, the less it appeals, but that's their lookout. (Guys, if you're reading this, go and see the film in advance so you're prepared for all the shocks.) A thought piece, or at least a 'hotly discussed' film, will do exactly that – feed you loads of stuff to discuss afterwards. Take a tip here from book-club members the world over – go on the Internet and memorise intelligent quotes and arguments which you can shamelessly pass off as your own later on.

REAL-LIFE DATE

'We were meeting up to go to the cinema, but because of the timings, we had to go to one in a really shitty part of town. Predictably, it was full of chav kids shouting and throwing things all the way through. It got unbearable after a while, and my date got up and screamed at them to be quiet, saying I'd beat them up if they carried on. They jeered at her and goaded me to have a go, which I was blatantly too scared to do, so she pulled out a rape alarm and fired it at the main troublemaker's face. They stopped the film and we had to run out. Never did get to know what happens at the end of *The Usual Suspects*...'

TOP TIP

If you ever go to a karaoke bar with a guy, make sure your performance is infused with sufficient irony. If you get tired and emotional and start showing off your best soprano, it will all end in tears. Karaoke is designed for piss-taking not for your knockout Celine Dion impression.

People complain that dates focused around a cultural event are a bad idea because you can't talk properly in a theatre/cinema. They're wrong. Sure you haven't talked, but when it's over, what better excuse to go for a drink to discuss the show. You have a mutual interest and a shared experience, so the chat will come flying.

The Activity Date

The activity date is where you meet up to do something physical – like a sport – and it is a much underused resource in dating circles. People naturally laugh at the idea, but think again! What quicker way could there be to work up a sweat together? And if you're pushed for time during the week because you need to get to the gym, it's a no-brainer. Ah, the sweet beauty of meeting the man of your dreams for some hearty fitness – killing two birds with one stone. And the advantages! Sport will be fun for once, you can rehydrate with alcohol and not only will you ogle their body with reckless abandon, but you also get to hear the noises they make during sex before making a decision. What's not to like?

Your initial concern will, of course, be how to conceal your minor imperfections beneath a suitably loose-fitting outfit. Don't want those muffin-tops poking out from the

TOP TIP

If you are getting into your car with a new man, be sure to have switched off the stereo at the end of your last excursion. It's difficult trying to explain how the *Dawson's Creek* soundtrack accidentally 'fell' into the CD player at full volume.

leotard now, do we? But halt that concealing reflex. He wants to see as much of you as possible. Why do you think guys join gyms? It's so that they can stand behind you on the running machine and gaze at your lovely arse.

And it doesn't need to be an ordinary sport. Sure you can meet for a game of tennis, or go jogging, but what if someone invited you paragliding or horse riding or scuba diving? How cool is that? Sports that might not be so conducive, though, are swimming (because it's just a bit weird), martial arts (although it's quite fun to fight on the first date), and curling (you will go off each other).

REAL-LIFE DATE

'I live near a place that does Laser Quest, and we thought it would be good "ironic" fun to go there for our first date. We turn up and it's nothing but young children and us. Fair enough, we think, should be easy killings. First we put on these vile sweat-drenched gimp-suits, then head into the arena. The children had clearly all agreed to pick on us, which they did, so we spent most of the time being shot at and having to return to base to "regenerate". Even worse, her gun didn't work so she couldn't shoot any of them in revenge. We eventually left the building stinking to high heaven and thoroughly pissed off. Neither of us saw the funny side, if indeed there was one.'

The big potential problem that overshadows all this, however, is a very dirty word. Competitivity. Yes, it's a big problem. All men are ruthlessly competitive, and can you honestly say you're not? A man will be absolutely furious if you beat him at tennis or ping-pong or anything for that matter, and he will resent you. Worse, he will be humiliated. And he will be especially put out if he thinks he's particularly good at said sport. So be prepared for this; if you beat him, he will never, ever forgive you. Surely this tried and tested formula rings a bell? You've reluctantly agreed to a game of cards or board game, only to end up winning, but the victory rings slightly hollow because the look in his eye says that you will be punished later. Losers, like elephants and mind-map users, never forget. So do you deliberately lose or play badly? Again no, because he's hoping to admire your sporting prowess. It's a double-edged sword; if you win, you lose and if you lose you lose. Either way you can't win. Safer therefore to be on the same side, like in mixed doubles or on the same five-a-side team (gulp).

TOP TIP

You've heard the rule about waiting three days before you call someone, and this is generally true. If things have gone amazingly well and they ask you to call the next day, text them. It's less of a gamble.

CHILLING STATISTIC

66% of doctors expect you not to be in contact with your ex

So they want you to surgically remove any trace of past relationships. Or at least not tell them when you go into remission.

The Home Date

'Come round to mine at eight and we'll take it from there!' A delightful proposition to be sure. Whether it's at yours or his, there's going to be an intimate dinner, bottles of wine, nosing around, and you both know it's only a short hop to the bedroom, which makes the evening all the more thrilling. It's an arena that can be controlled and is therefore ripe for manipulation. Anyway, there are so many dos and don'ts that it's easier to give them as a list.

At Yours:

- *Don't be ready when he arrives. Not only will that create the impression that you're not too fussed but it will allow you to enlist his help with the final touches in the kitchen – a strangely sexy experience.*

- *Do plant literature on the coffee table. You'll find that an unread but deliberately dog-eared copy of* A Brief History of Time *works wonders. He'll clock it and wham, instant admiration. If he asks any awkward questions, say, 'It's an ambitious work, but I'm not sure I agree with everything Professor Hawkins claims.' And you've hooked him. Later questions can be dodged by running into the kitchen because something's 'burning'.*

- *Don't bother with a starter. It looks like you've made too much effort. Main and pudding should do it. And don't reveal that you're trying a new recipe or that you've even used a cookbook; effortless culinary control is your brand.*

- *If you have a flatmate, get them out of the house. If you have to, bribe them. Cinema tickets and bucket of popcorn will suffice (although popcorn now costs £8 in some places!!!). Best of all make sure they don't come back late and interrupt proceedings. Flatmates are not subtle, even when they've been told to be.*

- *If you're choosing music to have in the background, resist the urge to simply slip on an Ibiza chill-out mix or the classical CD you got free with the Sunday papers. Music is a powerful weapon; the high-street stores exploit it, so must you.*

- *If your mother rings while he's there, sound really pleased to hear from her. True, she will be amazed and ask you what's wrong, but be really friendly as you steadily get her off the phone, as you are no doubt well practised. This will give the impression you rarely see her (a palpable relief for him) and that your family isn't too dysfunctional (more good news).*

- *This is perhaps a step to far, but possibly worth the effort. Select one of the framed photos on your mantelpiece/shelf/desk of any guy you know and turn it to face the wall. He will automatically sneak a look at it and casually ask who the person is. Then you can weave some bullshit story that it's your cousin who has joined a Jihad movement or is in prison for fraud or something dramatic. He will be immediately impressed. And relieved it's not your ex.*

- *Don't be too tidy. If the place looks like a show home, he'll be less inclined to make love to you on the living-room floor.*

- *If you have kept cuddly toys or a 'blankie' from your childhood, which enjoy pride of place on your pillow, I'm afraid now is the time to say goodbye to them. You knew this day would come, but face it: it hasn't come soon enough. There's a man on the scene, so 'Fluffy' must go into storage. The bed isn't big enough for both of them. Don't put those decorative girlie cushions on the bed either. It will make it look like you've slept alone since you left the nursery.*

- *Make sure you wipe any skid marks off the toilet bowl. He will be using the loo at some point.*

- *If he brings you flowers, make sure they go on the table. Guys like to mark their territory and think something they've spent money on has been put to good use. Alternatively, put them in your bedroom.*

- *After dinner, when you're innocently having drinks and 'sitting soft', your position is all important. Depending on whether you want to kiss him or not, you need to get yourself either into or out of a corner. You'll lead a merry dance around the sofa, with each trip to the loo allowing fine-tuning of the seating arrangements. But make no mistake about it, this is your theatre of conflict. It's crunch time on the sofa!*

- *Getting him to leave, if you don't want him to stay, requires some careful manoeuvring. Usually a simple, 'I've got to get up early…' and a look that says no should send him forlornly but considerately into the night. If you're feeling a bit jittery that he won't head off without a little more persuasion, suggest both going out for a nightcap at 'the bar round the corner'. Whether it's actually open or not is another matter, but the job is done.*

- *If you have a no-shoe policy at your gaff, it might be an idea to relax it for this special occasion. Or if you are unwilling to expose your floors to damage from his shoes, then coat the entire place with plastic sheeting and invite him to keep them on. Or borrow some shoe-covers from your local swimming pool.*

At His:

The three biggest rules are as follows:

- *Never, ever do a poo while you're there. Hold it in for another day.*

- *Don't touch his stereo. Ever. Not even to stroke it.*

- *And if you do go snooping and have a peep into his bedroom, do not look in his bedside drawer or in the shoebox under his bed. That is PRIVATE.*

Then:

- *Pick one of the artworks and express an interest. As a man he will not have given tremendous thought to decorating his walls, so will be flattered to hear he has natural good taste. Then ask him what that painting means and watch him squirm.*

- *Marvel at his gadgets. No matter how big his TV is, ask if it's a widescreen. Wonder at its accompanying hardware. 'What, a DVD player and a video recorder?' or 'You mean, it automatically records programmes and you just watch them when you want?' His pride and gratitude will prevent him from seeing your insincerity. He will love you.*

- *If you're bringing a bottle, don't worry about breaking the £5 barrier. You won't be drinking it yourself. Everything has been meticulously planned and coordinated; nothing left to chance. Your contribution will not feature in the proceedings. Alternatively arrive with a six-pack of beer, saying, 'I figured you'd have sorted out the wine, so these are for you for another time.' He'll be dead chuffed.*

- *Try and identify which one is* his *chair, both at the table and in the living room. Do not sit in it or he will malfunction.*

- *If you have specific dietary requirements, I'm afraid you must cast your mind back to the house rules of your childhood and* eat what you are given.

TOP TIP

If you ever are faced with the walk of shame one morning, be sure to borrow a coat or large jumper from him to preserve your modesty. That way you have an excuse to see him again to return it, or you can just keep it as proof for your friends.

Seven Deadly Sins of Dating

Pride	Don't ever presume it's in the bag
Envy	Don't give a moment's thought to his exes
Greed	Don't date more than one man at once
Gluttony	Don't be a fussy eater
Wrath	Don't lose sleep over a guy. Just ditch him and move on to the next
Sloth	Don't leave it all to him
Lust	Don't come on too strong

Movie kisses that nearly didn't happen 3: *Bridget Jones's Diary*

It's hard not to fall in love with Bridget Jones. She's fun, sexy, interesting, and, most of all, she's the real deal. No wonder she has eligible blokes fighting clumsily over her. Yet, she somehow fails to grasp her own appeal. She thinks her life is a complete disaster, and has an unshakeable paranoia that she is deeply unappealing.

Now the thing is, there are indeed some unappealing aspects to her. But they're not what she thinks they are. No one minds her being overweight (which, let's face it, she isn't), having verbal diarrhoea, wearing enormous pants, smoking and drinking to excess or making blue soup. We couldn't care less. And no one really minds the wealth of mildly irritating habits, such as referring to herself in the third person (which is defined by psychiatrists as an early indication of madness), and possessing no internal monologue, thereby providing an auto-commentary for her every thought and action.

What is genuinely quite annoying is that she's a little self-indulgent. And therein lies her problem. Hence the diary. You see Bridget wallows in her own singleness. In the title sequence we see her plonked in front of the TV in oversized pyjamas, drowning her sorrows in wine, stuffing her face and gently weeping at her misfortune. Fine, that might sound like a normal saturday night to you, but it can't be all that fun. She's a good catch, so why is she hiding herself away from the world of single men? Because her attitude to men is deferential. She believes she must wait until a man deigns to turn his attentions towards her. She doesn't take any steps of her own. Get out of the flat and go on the pull, Jones!

The profound mistake Bridget makes, and we've all done it, is to waste time with the roller-coaster thrills of the wrong person, when she could be enjoying the state of contentment and fulfilment with the right one. You know when you switch on the TV and settle on the first nonsense that appears, only to find out subsequently that you've missed something excellent on another channel because you hadn't bothered surfing in the first place. It's the same thing. Choosing too soon can throw you out of the game before it's even got started. And Hugh Grant is obviously a shit. It's her attachment to him that drives Colin Firth away and she's a fool for doing so. Remember the dinner scene, when Hugh Grant turns up. It's unbelievable that she doesn't tell him to sod off; she has the man she loves sat right there. No, she takes him on to the balcony for a secluded heart to heart. No wonder Firth buggers off.

On their weekend away, there's a controversial scene where it is implied that Hugh Grant and Bridget have just had anal sex. While this may be every man's fantasy, it is not an ideal means to encourage longevity in a relationship. Brilliant though one hears it is, shagging you up the arse is not the most romantic way of demonstrating one's affection. And let's face it, once he's done that, there are not many places he can go afterwards. Most people save it up for their tenth anniversary to inject a little excitement into proceedings. Imagine what he's going to do then... Vomit into you while two pigmies urinate on his bald patch? I'm not saying there's anything wrong with it, but don't expect him to call afterwards.

But she does a lot of things right. She dresses up super-tarty for a fancy dress party, she's confrontational with the man she loves, she's not afraid to dump people, she changes jobs and moves around a bit, and she's always herself. There's also the scene when she and Hugh Grant are lying in bed in post-coital bliss. She asks, 'Do you love me?' Richard Curtis makes a similar joke in *Four Weddings* and it's a good 'un. It correctly identifies that men have a deep-seated fear that if they sleep with a girl, she will fall in love with him. (This is perhaps the most inadvertently comic example of male arrogance.) Bridget plays it well by deliberately addressing the issue.

So Bridget gets it right in the end, but only by the skin of her teeth. Colin Firth is patient, but there's no telling what he'll do if he reads the rest of her diary.

PART FOUR

Keeping him

Seal the Deal

So you've met someone you like. You've been on a few dates. You've clicked. Hopefully, you have kissed him. What happens next? Well, if you're really keen on him, there'll be an overwhelming temptation to blurt everything out and confess exactly the way you feel. This is the real thing, after all, so you should sing it out to the hills while spinning round and round in a *Sound of Music* sort of way. Stop right there. Do not come clean at this point. If you reveal all, it will spoil the momentum and destroy the mystique. Keep your cards close to your chest. Don't let your guard down. There's a danger that if things move too fast, they will burn out. Reel him in slowly until he's under your spell, then enjoy the fruits of your labour. Indeed, the longer this 'uncertain' phase lasts, the more fun you'll have. So take your time about it and don't hurry. (Good rule of thumb: don't tell him you love him until after six months.)

In the early days you spend a lot of time being asked (and trying to figure out for yourself) if you're actually 'going out'. You know you're 'seeing each other' but that's not really good enough. You want official confirmation that you're an item. He probably does too. The trouble is the issue is never quite formally settled. Going out with someone just evolves. It does still happen, but the days of asking 'will you be my boyfriend?' are back with the pigtails, satchels and class hamster. Do not rush the day when you call him your boyfriend. It will give him a bit of a shock when it happens, so you need to wait long enough that it will be a pleasant one.

Much of your time initially is spent texting one another. Guys don't respond to texts as soon as they arrive. They wait for a convenient break and then respond to them all at once. So don't panic if you haven't heard anything in a while. He's composing a decent response. The

TOP TIP

What happens if you fart in front of him? It's bound to happen sometimes – statistics show you do it 13 times a day (and that's one more than the guys). He will be astounded, I guarantee you that, but his next reaction will betray how he sees you. If he laughs a lot, he likes you, if he looks totally horrified, he probably likes you even more, but if he goes silent, you're in trouble; he's doing some hasty re-evaluation.

perfect text message contains only two things. A suggestion of a means to meet up and a gag, in that order. 'Hey there, do you want to go and see…' followed by either a new joke or a reference to an old one. And don't say 'Hope the meeting/theatre/dinner went well' too much as it suggests you've been thinking about him all day. Keep texts short and sweet. Be casual.

TOP TIP
It's not that good an idea to send a man flowers. Even if an extraordinary event/ achievement demands it, avoid a bouquet. Men feel very uneasy about this territory.

The ancient bus rule (the one in which you wait ages then several come along, etc.) originated from the end of singleness. You go from periods of great drought to an abundance of choice. You're taken and suddenly everyone wants a piece of you. It's amazingly flattering and you want to tell the world. It's quite tempting to tell your new man about all the attention too. But guys really don't like to think you're having to choose between different men. Same as you, they expect to be treated either as the only option or not an option at all. So the best tactic if he suspects others are on your case is to complain that you're receiving unwelcome attention. Your phone goes and you groan, 'This guy just won't get the message.' Brilliant move, he'll be flattered that you're officially rejecting other offers, but mildly impressed that you're so in demand. But don't go on about your suitors. Well, maybe once or twice is all right.

'Are we staying at yours or mine tonight?' is the question that begins to crop up soon enough and may prove your first sticking point. Men are very lazy, so even though your home may be a lot nicer, he will try and find reasons why his is better or the more logical place to stay. Resist his efforts; keep it an even split. He's testing the waters to see if he can get away with having things his way. This is a profound moral battle: be strong.

What if your new man lives far away, or even worse, suddenly has to move away? Will that inevitably scupper your plans? Well, long-distance relationships are really hard. The usual pattern is late-night phone calls when you're both tired and have no news to report, and weekends together where the pressure of using every second to the full invariably causes rows. And it is only viable as a temporary measure. Unfortunately, in the early stages of romance, neither

TOP TIP

Men love the idea of coming to 'save' you when you're ill. Why you would want to be visited when you look like death warmed up is beyond me, but let them do it and they'll feel good about themselves.

of you are in a position to make demands on the other. But soon enough you are going to have to have a little chat along the lines of, 'things are going really well, perhaps we should discuss what our long-term plans are geographically, because it would be nice to move things forward'.

Whatever you do, don't issue an ultimatum. It is frustrating when it feels like a job takes precedence over your relationship, but a job is inflexible, whereas you can both adapt.

In the first month, if he's not sure about you, don't force the issue. If he's still not sure about you after two, cut him loose. It's not worth the temporary release of getting involved with someone who is coming from a radically different direction. Whatever you're after, whether it's a fling, a relationship to tide you over or something serious, make sure he's looking for the same thing. Or there will be tears somewhere down the line.

Meet the Friends

When you are introduced to his friends, you come under such microscopic scrutiny that they may as well give you a full medical probe. The chummy, welcoming atmosphere conceals the fact that your every thought, word and deed is under constant scrutiny. In fact, they may as well fetch an organ grinder and force you to do a dance. All the while you have to focus on your new man, exuding signals that you're a hot new item, but without seeming too keen or clingy. You are there to perform, and your performance must be worthy of global acclaim. Of course, the same thing applies to him when he meets your friends, so there is some justice in the world. But for both parties, this is no picnic.

Now here's the really tricky part. It is very important to a guy that his best friends think you're cool. For cool, read any one of funny, interesting or, dare I say, fit. Fit, you scream? But that's lunacy! Yes, and it's also immature, superficial and crude but these are men, for goodness' sake, and such is the nature of the beast. So you need to be quite flirty with them I'm afraid; but flirty in the way you would be with a bank manager discussing your loan or your boss during appraisals or your dad when you've crashed his car. Not flirty enough for them to fully notice or to hurt his manly pride, but enough that they'll be envious of their friend. This envy is exactly what he hopes for, it's the reason he's parading you before them. He thinks you're great and their approval will set that in stone.

So can your pride stoop to such an act? Surely if they're not going to like you, that's their problem, no? An admirable attitude, but think what it means to you when your friends don't like a new guy. Their combined disapproval can stop a fledgling romance in its tracks. The approval of his social circle is crucial, most of all at the vulnerable early stages. Console yourself that years from now, when things are nice and settled, you can admit to him that you think they're a bunch of twats. He'll probably agree. But for now, their gladiatorial thumbs-up or thumbs-down is a life or death sentence.

During this ordeal, his friends will try and make him look as bad as possible. Jokes about his sexuality, manhood and job are common territory among real 'lads' but clever-er types still won't be able to resist the odd subtly coded dig. So if he looks beleaguered during proceedings, don't be surprised, try not to take offence and don't leap to his defence. This is their form of grooming. They do it for the same reasons your friends try and make you look *good*.

Both genders on these occasions cannot resist the urge to recount lengthy stories about the 'hilarious' exploits of their friends whom no one else has never heard of. This can render such evenings tedious. If you're with your friends, a stern look and possibly even a mild rebuke will get things back on the straight and narrow, but if it's his friends, and men are terrible at this, you can but grin and bear it. Men find their own anecdotes so hysterical here, they'll be flattered if you laugh along. 'You mean, he woke up in his own piss?! How droll.' Sorry, we all have our crosses to bear.

Quite often the combined nerves and anxiety of trying to impress fosters an insatiable thirst for alcohol. Do not get pissed. The number of anecdotes that do the rounds about these situations descending into drunken shame is astounding. Most people's 'puke' anecdotes start with 'I was really trying to impress someone…' Don't get over excited.

Meet the Parents

Meeting his parents is a whole new level of scrutiny. Not quite so important to acquire their approval as the friends', because parental endorsement can be the kiss of death to many relationships. But parents can deliberately make life very difficult for you if they feel you're not good enough for their darling boy.

The father's approval should come easily enough; just demonstrate a keen interest in his conversation and an enthusiasm for his pet subjects. Then sit back and enjoy the plaudits. 'Such a fascinating girl,' 'Really has strong opinions,' 'Wonderful catch!' Yup, flatter Dad and he'll be yours for ever. The mother is a different matter. She'll be waiting for you to trip up. Dressed in a revealing manner, not helpful enough, drinking too much – all are blunders that she is waiting for you to commit. But remember that her fatal weakness is her son: if you talk about him incessantly and in glowing terms, she too will fall in love with you.

If you are going to take them a present when you visit, avoid wine, because the more money you've spent on it, the less likely they are to let you drink it yourself. Get a pot plant. Subtler than a bunch of flowers, the plant will maintain a benign presence in their house, reminding them continually of your generosity and sweet fragrance. Unfortunately, when it begins to wither and die, the mother will see it as a terrible omen, unequivocally prefiguring the demise of your relationship.

When you introduce him to your parents, it goes without saying that you give them a pre-emptive bollocking to prevent them saying anything embarrassing. Parents have a fondness for recounting endearing little stories about your childhood eccentricities, so ban them from talking about you in any way. Father's find it hard not to make little digs now and then, like a 'Oh, I wouldn't sit on *that* sofa, she once peed on it when she was five years old.' I guess they feel the money they've spent on you entitles them to do something at your expense once in a while. And expressly forbid your parents from showing your baby photos. When they reach for the family albums, reach for the door handle.

The Mini-Break

A mini-break is often the first confirmation that you're officially going steady. And what could be better than fleeing your well-rehearsed routine for a few days when the expense of ordering room service at breakfast time is worth it and you can idle away the hours in blissful relaxation with a hot new guy? Relaxation? Think again, honey. You are not here to relax. You are here to step up the campaign to a new level. You'll pack your best clothes and pretend that you wear them normally, be friendly to everyone you meet, even if you don't like them, and ruthlessly overrule your every fault and defect. Positivism exudes from your every pore. You're perfect.

But the weekend away is actually more of a test of how you both cope under pressure, because there will be travel involved, and an ability to travel smoothly together is a golden endorsement of your compatibility. So whether you're going to a nice B& B in the magnificent British countryside or increasing your carbon footprint with a gratuitous overseas jaunt (UK tourism rules, OK!), you'll need to get there. And things can go so wrong on the way.

Also, hopefully he's tailored the weekend to your needs – a lovely spa break, or a secluded beach holiday or a gastronomic tour – but there's just a chance he'll want to hike you up a mountain or take you sea kayaking. It's not meant vindictively, he's not even being selfish – he probably thinks you'll love it – but part of him wants to take you for a test drive and see if you can handle it. Performing well in these physical tasks will stand you in good stead for ever and if the challenge is completed without complaint, you have passed the test. So if you like the guy, you just have to smile through gritted teeth this once, knowing you need never do it again. Later attempts for outward bound breaks can be skilfully side-stepped. If you *really* don't want to participate, though, feign injury. Be warned though; it had better be a pretty severe injury.

Worse still to come, and this is no delicate matter, but a weekend away together may be the first time you unavoidably have to take a dump in each other's vicinity. Hitherto, a man may have prospered under the illusion that a good lady such as yourself was not capable of such base acts. This might be the occasion when a nicely timed whopper disabuses him of the fallacy.

TOP TIP

Wait until he's out of the room before you stuff the bathroom freebies into your handbag. Guys can never understand why you would want to do this.

Bonking

Just so you know, there are five acknowledged bases as a couple get down to it.

Base 1: *Snogging*
Base 2: *Heavy petting over the clothing to sexual zones*
Base 3: *Manual relief*
Base 4: *Oral relief*
Base 5: *Doing it!!!! Woo hoo!*

Now it is usually accepted that there is a steady progression down these ranks to the heavenly Base 5, though some may prefer to save Base 4 till last, something about a question of intimacy. Some guys might even say that there is a Base 6, reserved for Christmas and birthdays, but this is unofficial and should be approached with the utmost discretion.

Anyway, how soon should you sleep with someone? General guidelines are: immediately if you never intend to see him again. Wait a little longer if you like him. That may seem the wrong way round, but it works for many. Obviously, sleeping with someone greatly increases the chances of getting hurt – the same thing happens to men, believe it or not – so discretion is advised and waiting usually pays off in the long run. You can't unshag someone if you've already done it, but there's always a shag to look forward to if you haven't.

CHILLING STATISTIC

33% of musicians will not respect you afterwards once you've given them a blow job

Maybe it's because they're accustomed to groupie love, but peel off their leather trousers too soon, and you're unlikely to have the next love ballad written about you.

Now modern magazines have made the point that women are entitled to orgasms, and men accept this, indeed welcome it. More female orgasms means an increase in demand and therefore supply. So far so good. But the proliferation of pornography has somewhat dulled men's concept of what constitutes sexual normalcy and what women want. Deep down he will want you to speak in an American accent, do some lesbo, wear high heels at all times, scream like a banshee and insist upon a money shot on your breasts and/or face after you've been spit-roasted and DPed (don't ask). He does not think this porn fantasy is unreasonable, despite the fact that he himself is unable to provide the twelve-inch cock and Zeus-like body. You need to come down hard on this juvenility straight away (snigger, snigger!).

TOP TIP

If you carry your own condoms around, will he think you're a slag? No, he'll be delighted and relieved that the usual awkwardness can be neatly side-stepped.

If a man falls asleep after making love to you, it does not signify a lack of respect. It doesn't mean he feels nothing, or is revolted by the experience or bored of you already. He is exhausted. He is 'shagged out'. Give him space to breathe and he'll come slinking back like an Andrex puppy with an erection.

TOP TIP

If you're pretty confident you won't be coming home one night, it's fairly acceptable to take a toothbrush with you. But don't take your wash kit – that feels like you're moving in.

A guy may insist on keeping the lights on during bonking when you would far rather remain under cover of darkness. Basically, you get to choose.

The reason he wants the lights on is because it's incredibly sexy seeing you naked, not so he can appraise you. He's a man, not one of your friends. Don't give a moment's thought to your wobbly bits now: they're meant to wobble – you're being shagged senseless after all.

TOP TIPS

Don't be fooled into thinking the rest of the world is busy having marathon sex sessions, while you aren't. People have sex a lot less frequently than you might imagine.

Conclusion

Being single is not an incomplete state – you're not dependent on the presence of a man to be fulfilled and you never will be. Society may conspire to make you feel that way, but it simply isn't so. Nor is it a life sentence or some form of predetermined burden in life. If you do want a man, then you need only make the effort to look for one. Being single means everything lies ahead of you and you get to make all the choices.

The reason men and women have negative conceptions being single is because the path to pulling is an unpredictable one, beset with soaring highs and plunging lows. It's extremely easy to have your confidence eroded when you set about trying to pull because, like everything else in life, it doesn't always work out first time. But never forget that guys are just as apprehensive as you are. You both want the same thing and have the same trouble finding it.

When you do meet someone, it's funny when you look back over your courting days and can't believe all the trouble you both went too – the crap flirting, the muddled kisses, the misconstrued texts – when it was so obvious you liked each other from the start. Over time, men and women have devised a mating ritual infinitely more protracted and complicated than any other creature on earth. But unlike many creatures on earth (apart from swans and gibbons), when we get it right, we stay together for a lifetime. So the struggle is worth it. Pulling is simple but it still requires you to make a real effort and potentially reap a lifetime of reward.

The hardest part will be locating someone you like. But you only have to change your routine a tiny amount to start meeting new people. Or be bolder. Change jobs, live somewhere new, do anything to break out of your current circle, which consists of no one you fancy. Ask yourself this question. Do I fancy anyone I know? If so, then do something about it. If you don't, then you need to cast your net wider until you find someone you like.

And don't be disheartened if you only meet dickheads. Of course you will; the planet is full of them. Just switch on Channel 4 and you'll see that. It's too easy to give up before you've even begun. You need to ruthlessly scour the planet, like Daniel Day Lewis in *The Last of the Mohicans*, and have a damn good time doing so. And you don't need quantity, just quality. Identify who you really like and go for it, guns blazing. If it doesn't work out, move on. You don't need to beat yourself up and overanalyse why things didn't work out, they just didn't. There's someone else round the corner.

A final thought. This book and countless others advise of all the tactics to employ and tricks to play to get the man of your dreams, and maybe that rings somewhat hollow. Surely there's a more romantic way of finding your soulmate? We all dream of meeting someone wonderful and for that initial connection to do away with the need for games and tactics. We want love to carry us through. And, yes, this does happen. But it doesn't have to be that way. A reasonable analogy – though perhaps a corny one – might be a sailing ship. Without the wind, it cannot move, but a ship does not rely on wind alone. (I know that I'm beginning to sound like Paulo Coelho here.) No, it requires all manner of fine-tuning to make it glide on smoothly. So it is with the art of pulling. You need to steer yourself in the right direction while the forces of nature help you on your way.

So good luck and enjoy the thrill of the chase. The perfect guy for you is out there somewhere right now. Put down this book and go get him.

Troubleshooting Guide

He hasn't called	Wait four days then assume the worst. If you have his number, send him a text in a week. Don't hang around – he hasn't lost your number.
He's not returning your calls	Pull the rip cord. If a guy hasn't returned two of your calls, don't call again. True he might have lost his phone but if he really likes you he'll track you down somehow.
He was crap in bed	Give him a second chance. He might have been nervous/ drunk/ too turned on or any other of a myriad of reasons. However disappointed you were, he'll be feeling a million times worse. Give it another chance and it may well exceed your expectations.

	After all, you didn't like coffee the first time you had it.
He flirts with everyone	The hallmark of insecurity. It doesn't necessarily mean he's not into you – he may well be doing it because he thinks you're not into him – but he wants your attention. If you ask him to stop, it will flatter his ego. Storm out if he goes overboard, or give him a taste of his own medicine. Find someone he hates and drape yourself over them.
He's wonderful but his friends are a bunch of dicks	Not fair to judge a book by its cover (especially this one!). Many friends endure simply due to longevity. He may also think they're dicks, but time has bound them firmly together. Time will hopefully also prise them apart.

He's still close to his ex	Never ideal. And if they went out for years it's especially bad. The key is why they split up. Best possible scenario is that they slowly drifted apart because it means there's no unfinished business. The rule is: the longer they were together, the longer they should be tolerated being in contact afterwards. But if you suspect one still holds a torch, intercede! Avoid direct confrontation – everything will always be denied – just use your feminine guile to undermine their fragile bond.
He insists you're 'just seeing each other'	Classic inability to commit. This guy is keeping his options open, having his cake and eating it. He likes you but he doesn't care about you, which is fine if you feel the same way. Just be aware that he will trade you in for

	another model as soon as one comes along. And let slip that you regard yourself as still single; that might shock him into making his mind up.
He has quite a past	Not much you can do about this, sadly. It suggests that he'll know what makes you tick, he has evolved the ability to make a decent choice and he's coming in with his eyes open.
He hasn't much experience with girls	Schooling your adult lover in the ways of the flesh can be quite sweet or quite off-putting. You have a blank canvas, so you can mould him to your precise specifications.
He might be gay	It would be tempting to shag his brains out to see if you can hang a prized 'conversion' trophy on your belt. But it's

	not going to happen. And beware the pyrrhic victory of taming his sexuality. After 25 years of marriage, he'll probably dump you for a young boy.
His best friend is a girl	You must find out if they have a history. And if not, why not? If there is some unrequited love there, neutralise the threat, while maintaining the illusion of friendship. Say how much you like her. Only then can you start doing your research.
He sends slightly inappropriately filthy texts	It's alarming when someone spoils the romantic stirrings of a fledgling text relationship with overly sexual messages. Does he only want you for sex? Maybe so. Decide what you're after and text back accordingly.

He still lives with his parents	The premise of many a comedy, but not a particularly amusing scenario in reality. It means he's either poor, lazy, emotionally vulnerable or all three. Is he really 'between homes'? Stress the unacceptability of the arrangement. Go on strike and refuse to visit him there.
He's too keen	Very, very difficult situation. You really like him, but, for goodness' sake, if only he could stop coming on so suffocatingly strong. Yes, this is the age-old double-edged sword. If you tell him to back off, he'll think you don't like him and get keener. If you don't say anything, his eagerness will drive you away. Just be honest with him. Say you really like him but ask to take things a bit slower. If this is done with the right

	amount of reassurance, it will work.
His mother doesn't like me	Don't worry too much. Unless he still lives at home or comes from a deeply religious family, this shouldn't be a problem. If his mother is overbearing, turn this to your advantage by presenting yourself as a welcome antidote. He might see you as an irresistible act of rebellion. If she continues to cause trouble after a significant period, don't slag her off. Just console yourself that if you get married, you'll sit her next to the deaf vicar at the reception.
He's hiding something from me	Guys are as good at not telling the whole truth as you are at detecting it. If you have that nagging sensation – your Spider Senses are tingling –

	that something's not right, you're probably right. Trouble is, if you ask him, he'll deny everything. He's probably married, cheating on you, living a double life as a Soviet agent, whatever. Trust your instinct. Stop calling him.
He only calls me when he's drunk	Get out fast. Yes, you give him the horn, which is flattering, but what does it say when he needs eight pints of Stella before he can engage with you? Use him for sex, if you so choose, but only if you can cleanly dislocate your body from your heart and soul.
He's behaving as if he actively wants me not to like him	He's trying to make you dump him. The man doesn't have the nerve to call it off so he wants you to do it for him. A 'let's call it a day' from you is all he's waiting for. Just stop calling him.

He works so hard we hardly get to see each other	Not spending enough time together is a huge problem for couples, and it's harder at the beginning because you don't yet feel entitled to demand his time, and asking for any more feels like nagging. Set up frequent concrete fixtures – dinners, films, gigs, etc – so that he will actively make the time for you. He will be less inclined to leave work for a nebulous 'Shall we meet up?'
He's perfect and you're sure you will mess it up	Don't panic. When things go well, you're just waiting for the inevitable obstacle to come and spoil it. There's a temptation to pre-empt that by running it aground yourself. Do not confess all your feelings for him. Just sit tight and keep your shit together. He's probably thinking the same thing himself.

Also available from Vermilion

Why Mr Right Can't Find You... and How to Make Sure He Does

J M Kearns

Why Mr Right Can't Find You... exposes the classic myths of dating and reveals the surprising secrets of true compatibility, giving you the tools to eliminate the Mr Wrongs and, more importantly, recognise the perfect man for you. No more playing games or second-guessing, with this book you will discover that any time is the right time to meet Mr Right, that on-line dating can be the most successful way to find a partner and, above all, that your ideal mate is out there now, looking for you. You just have to go to the right places...

Witty and down-to-earth, this practical guide will turn everything you thought you knew about mating and dating on its head.

Why Women Talk and Men Walk

Patricia Love and Steven Stosny

You know how it can get when a relationship turns sour. Women want to talk things through. Men want to walk away and ignore the problem. It's an uncomfortable scenario that we've all witnessed or experienced, and one that we'd like to avoid.

By explaining that it is the fundamental differences between men and women that can make relationships so hard, authors Patricia Love and Steven Stosny reveal that the key to a great relationship is not communication but rediscovering and maintaining the connection a couple felt when they first met. Their groundbreaking techniques show how to engage with a partner and reignite the feelings that made that partnership so special to begin with.

☐ Why Mr Right Can't Find You… 9780091917098 £7.99

☐ Why Women Talk and Men Walk 9780091917104 £9.99

FREE POSTAGE AND PACKING

Overseas customers allow £2.00 per paperback

BY PHONE: 01624 677237

BY POST: Random House Books

c/o Bookpost, PO Box 29, Douglas

Isle of Man, IM99 1BQ

BY FAX: 01624 670923

BY EMAIL: bookshop@enterprise.net

Cheques (payable to Bookpost) and credit cards accepted

Prices and availability subject to change without notice.

Allow 28 days for delivery.

When placing your order, please mention if you do not wish to receive any additional information.

www.rbooks.co.uk